Strategic Humanism

STRATEGIC HUMANISM

Lessons on Leadership from the Ancient Greeks

Claudia Hauer

Political Animal Press
Toronto • Chicago

Political Animal Press

www.politicalanimalpress.com

Distributed by the University of Toronto Press

www.utpdistribution.com

Cataloguing data available from Library and Archives Canada

ISBN 978-1-895131-44-4 (paperback)

ISBN 978-1-895131-45-1 (ebook)

Typeset in Garamond and Lato

Printed and bound in Canada

Contents

Acknowledgments

I am grateful to St. John's College in Santa Fe, for granting me leave of absence to spend time over the last decade at the U.S. Air Force Academy as a visiting professor. My heartfelt gratitude goes to the Department of Philosophy and the Department of English and Fine Arts at the U.S. Air Force Academy for hosting me so generously and with such kindness, and for creating the haven from which this manuscript emerged. I thank Political Animal Press for creating this venue for authors who are trying to link theory and practice, something that is so needed in our world.

The author's opinions do not reflect the official position of the U.S. Air Force Academy or the Department of Defense.

For my husband Jim, who has always believed in me.

Introduction

The first class I taught at the Air Force Academy, in 2010, was an introduction to Greek classics, and included the historian Thucydides' *History of the Peloponnesian War*. At the beginning of the second class, as we prepared to discuss our reading in Thucydides' work, a cadet challenged me: 'Why do we still read this?" His two-fold point was clear: not only was this a suspiciously ancient text, but in addition, the big war strategies that Thucydides describes had not been employed in warfare by the United States since Operation Desert Storm in 1991. Counterinsurgency, not big war, was a more popular topic in strategic circles in 2010. Was Thucydides still a relevant part of an American military officer's education? We made a deal. If I couldn't show them something of contemporary relevance in Thucydides' work by the end of the class, I would replace it with something that had more immediate appeal. Long story short, we stuck with Thucydides.

Regardless of whether we are in an age of big war, my cadets and I discovered that Thucydides describes a cycle of human violence still easily recognizable in today's news headlines. Thucydides' text may not be the best source for studying current military tactics, but it remains an excellent source for understanding the principles of human conflict that form the basis of strategy. "Strategy is difficult, but we do not need to rediscover how to do it," asserts United States Air Force Brigadier General Scott Bethel, "Planners and senior leaders should be steeped in the liberal arts."[1]

In his 2002 book, *Warrior Politics: Why Leadership Demands a Pagan Ethos*, the journalist Robert Kaplan concludes that "As future crises arrive in steep waves, our leaders will realize that the world is not "modern" or "postmodern" but only a continuation of the ancient – a world that, despite its technologies, the best Chinese, Greek, and Roman philosophers would have understood and known how to navigate."[2] Kaplan's work illustrates connections between ancient and modern, and make it clear that the classics remain relevant for today's leaders. The essays in this book are intended similarly to illustrate how we can read the Greek classics both seriously for their own sake, and also with an eye to their continued relevance. In order to learn the lessons we need to learn about the timeless aspects of conflict, we need to adopt this integrated way of reading these ancient texts. In this context, we are not looking for an academic answer to the question Why do we still read this?, but rather attempting to explore the connection between ancient and modern in more practical terms of leadership and decision-making. These essays study some of the ways that the characters and scenarios found in the texts of Homer, Herodotus, Thucydides and Aristotle continue to arise today in ways that do not so much replicate the originals, but reference them, in the spirit of Mark Twain's observation that history doesn't repeat itself; it rhymes.

1   Bethel, Scott, Prupas, Aaron, Ruby, Tomislav and Michael Smith. 2010. "Change Culture, Reverse Careerism." *Joint Forces Quarterly* 58, 3rd quarter 2010: 82-88.

2   Kaplan, Robert. 2002. *Warrior Politics: Why Leadership Demands a Pagan Ethos.* New York: Vintage Books, 16.

Many of the readers of this book will have come of age in the midst of e-readers and smart phones. The digital generations are subjected to the pervasive social expectation that there are technological solutions, not just to problems of engineering and science, but to all humanity's problems. The media bombards us with mechanical resources - digital devices, prescription drugs, and others – that are supposed to solve all 'lifestyle' problems. This social environment is profoundly Cartesian, that is to say, post-Hellenic. The rise of the social sciences has been predicated on the assumption that the human dimensions of political and social behavior can be quantified in ways that will make them receptive to mechanical, quantifiable solutions. In this Cartesian climate, it remains the humanities, through offering direct access to works of literature, philosophy and history that are "substantially and methodologically unbounded" by the quantifiable methods of science, that can preserve their access to the whole spectrum of the human condition.[3]

The Greek texts that form the basis for this collection of essays belong to a substantial Greek humanist tradition. Greek humanism reflects an interest in the human as a whole being, possessing some inseparable combination of rational and irrational qualities. This Greek humanism is not to be confused with the rational humanism of the Enlightenment, which separated reason from its corporeal backdrop of emotion and imagination, or with humanitarianism,

---

3 Hill, Christopher. *Grand Strategies: Literature, Statecraft, and World Order.* 2010. New Haven: Yale University Press, 6-7. Christopher Hill goes on to write: "Literature can capture the multifarious whole. This is all the more necessary in our time because of the hegemony of the social sciences, particularly political science, which by self-definition must confine itself to a narrow band of problems capable of scientifically replicable solutions – leaving the biggest questions beyond its reach."

a concept introduced by Francis Bacon, which excludes the irrational emotions and appetites, and focuses on how pure reason can improve the physical quality of life. Greek humanism focuses on our way of being human, and our way of exercising the synthesis of our capacities. This Greek humanism does not aim at some abstract notion of humanity, but at our individual way of being. As such, Greek humanism should resonate strongly today. As this book goes to print, the novel coronavirus has profoundly disrupted business as usual around the world. Individuals have had to come to a reckoning with their assumptions about what it means to be human in an age in which technology has so far not succeeded in eradicating the problem that threatens us.

Reinhold Niebuhr, in his critique of America's misguided desire to exercise control over history on a global scale, concludes that the Cartesian climate has contributed to America's sense that it can reduce history to a science. Niebuhr writes:

> It is particularly true of the host of modern social, psychological or anthropological scientists, who think it an easy matter to match the disinterestedness of the natural scientist in the field of historical values. They all forget that, though man has a limited freedom over the historical process, he remains immersed in it. None of them deal profoundly with the complex "self" whether in its individual or in its collective form. This self has a reason; but its reason is more intimately related to the anxieties and fears, the hopes and ambitions of the self as natural organism than the "pure" reason of the natural scientist...[4]

4   Niebuhr, Reinhold. 2008. *The Irony of American History*. Chicago: University of Chicago Press, 82.

The first essay in this volume, on the enormous influence of the 16th and 17th century writers Francis Bacon and René Descartes on modern problem solving, is intended to give the reader a background against which to integrate the lessons of Greek humanism into the landscape of the technocratic social sciences. We need to be able to see the technocratic argument for what it is in order to understand the resources that Greek humanism can bring to strategic development. In this first essay, I lay out the pitfalls of applying a technocratic approach to solving problems that require recognition of what Niebuhr calls above the "complex self." The Greeks, by contrast, took it for granted that a human being will bring all of his or her faculties to decision making – reason, intuition, imagination, emotion, and sometimes even the raw appetites. The complexity of many human decision-making processes should not be masked or oversimplified by overlooking key human factors that may be involved.

This book is intended to familiarize the reader with a Hellenic way of seeing the world, in which character displays itself in action, not in contemplation. Active individuals must make decisions and act without knowing everything about the situation. Their decisions are made not from narrow, scientific analysis of specific data, but from their holistic ability to take in and sum up a complex situation in which "everything counts," and "a purely rational or technocratic approach is likely to lead one astray."[5] In studying characters such as Achilles, Croesus, Cyrus, and others, a small detail can be as informative as the large outcome. As the ancient Greek bibliographer Plutarch writes,

5   Hill, *Grand Strategies*, 21, 7.

The most glorious exploits do not always furnish us with the clearest discoveries of virtue or vice in men; sometimes a matter of less moment, an expression or a jest, informs us better of their characters and inclinations than the most famous sieges, the greatest armaments, or the bloodiest battles whatsoever.[6]

In the Greek literature, small incidents and interactions often reveal aspects of a character that are symbolic of the whole of his life. The particulars are more important here than conclusions. The focus is on the behavior of real people and states, and our texts are as much works of literature and history as philosophy. The topic here is more about people than abstract ideas, and is intended to acquaint us with individuals. My intent is to bring these characters to life as much as I can, for their way of being in the world has a lot to offer our understanding of our own times. I don't present themes abstractly, but rather focus on the life choices that face these dramatic characters, and the changing circumstances in which they made their choices, in order to show how and why we can identify with these characters, and continue to learn from their stories.

The Greek texts presented here span many hundreds of years. Homer's *Iliad* was passed down orally for centuries before it was written down in the 6th or 5th centuries BCE. The Greek historians Herodotus and Thucydides wrote during the 5th century BCE, and the Greek philosopher Aristotle during the 4th. As such, these texts reflect the transition of Greek society from its youth to its maturity, and into the Athenian decline. The shift I am most interested in during these centuries is the development of the idea of human

---

6 Plutarch. 2001. "Life of Alexander," in *Plutarch's Lives Volume II*. Translated by John Dryden. New York: Modern Library, 139.

as an autonomous agent who can bring all of his or her qualities
to the management of his or her own affairs. I call this Greek
humanism, both to distinguish it from Enlightenment humanism, which focuses on the importance of scientific reason, and
also to acknowledge the emerging power captured in these texts
of a human individual who can wield both rational and irrational
powers to great effect.

In choosing to focus on Homer, Herodotus, Thucydides, and
Aristotle, I do not intend to be dismissive of the Greek philosopher
Plato's extraordinary contribution to philosophy and the history
of ideas. This contribution is self-evident, and not in question
here. Much of what will follow will draw on Plato in diverse ways.
However, one key aspect of Plato's work was a turn toward idealism, which runs counter to the particular species of humanism that
is my topic. Plato gives voice to the possibility that human affairs
are flawed reflections of perfect supranatural ideals. This was by
no means the only substantial contribution that Plato made to
philosophy, and in the essays that follow, I draw freely on many
of Plato's other contributions. In particular, Plato's commitment
to dialogue is very important here, and also his engagement with
the so-called tripartite human soul (a soul seen as made up of
appetites and passions, as well as reason). The texts we will explore
here are interested in ways of conceiving of the human being as an
integrated bundle of reason, emotions, and desires. While Plato's
rational idealism has looked less radical since the Enlightenment,
Plato's strict separation of reason and emotion has not always been
credible to classical scholars. The classicist E. R. Dodds, for example, is critical of this bias in favor of isolated reason, marveling that

Socrates and Plato can "dismiss so easily the part played by emotion in determining ordinary behavior."[7]

In order for the Greeks to get serious about philosophy, as they clearly were by the time of Plato and Aristotle, they needed a strong sense of the interpretive potential of language. As we shall see, this could not develop until the individual was free to shape and control his social environment. In Homer's *Iliad*, we will see the earlier world in which the individual was not 'integrated' but 'disintegrated', a world in which unity of mind, body, and soul was impossible. Aristotle was free to explore the parameters of human morality in the 4th century BCE because other Greek authors had already set a precedent for experimenting with the art of interpretation. The two Greek historians from this time, Herodotus and Thucydides, played an important role in shaping Greek as a literary language. In his account of the Persian Wars (the Persians' two successive invasions of Greece in the early 5th century BCE), Herodotus spends most of his first book documenting the emergence of a spirit of individualism in Greece and Asia Minor (today's Middle East). Individuals were able to amass power on a large scale because they had the ability and the autonomy to manipulate the interpretive power of language. Although many of these characters used force as well as persuasion to get their way, the art of persuasion was developing as a political and military tool. Thucydides, in his account of the Peloponnesian War at the end of the 5th century BCE, draws attention to his own capacity for interpretation when he acknowledges the lack of technologies that could record critical

---

7   Dodds, E. R. 1951. *The Greeks and the Irrational*. Berkeley: University of California Press, 185.

historical speeches verbatim. Because "it was… difficult to carry them word for word in one's memory," Thucydides tells us he had to insert some of his own interpretive perspective as well: "my habit has been to make the speakers say what in my opinion was demanded of them by the various occasions" (1. 22).

Thanks to Thucydides' willingness to exercise his interpretive judgment, we have access not just to data about the Peloponnesian War, but to a reflection on how the ideological conflict between Athens and Sparta originated and developed. Thucydides' willingness to subject the raw material of history to the organizing principles of reason, while maintaining a healthy respect for the role of the irrational in human affairs, sets a precedent for an integrated approach to the art of presenting human leadership in human terms.

Together, the two historians paint a compelling picture of the emergence and decline of Athenian democracy. Herodotus shows us the development of the arts of interpretation and persuasion in practical life. The hallmark of democracy, namely the free use of speech for political persuasion, was associated by Herodotus with Athens' acquisition of power. Although the art of political persuasion enabled democracy to flourish in Greece, Thucydides shows us how rhetoric becomes a political liability as the Athenians allow themselves to be persuaded to neglect their best interests and undertake an ambitious and aggressive military campaign to conquer Sicily. During the early days of the Iraq War, one of my colleagues made up a bumper sticker that drew attention to the parallels between these two invasions. Ironically imitating the popular "Invade Iraq? No!" bumper sticker, his read "Invade Sicily? No!" A popular symbol for its nation's hubris, the Sicilian expedition has come to be read recently against the backdrop of the military campaigns in Vietnam, Iraq, and Afghanistan. In Thucydides' so-called Melian Dialogue, the breath-taking arrogance of the Athenian rhetoric displays how easily a democracy at home can become tyrannical and aggressive in its foreign policy.

In the moral vacuum left by Athens' defeat in the Peloponnesian war, moral philosophy was born in Greece, through the person of Socrates, and the written work of Plato and Aristotle. While Plato approached the problems of morality from a theoretical perspective, Aristotle made an effort to see how morality could be achieved in practice. The final essay in this volume will take up the ethical model developed by Aristotle. Although it came too late to save the Athenians from their hubris, Aristotle's theory of morality addresses a deficiency in 5th century BCE Greek society, namely that it provided few coherent models for how to achieve virtue in one's own conduct. Aristotle's work is a culmination of Greek humanism, in that it accepts that humans are irrational as well as rational, yet it offers a model for how to integrate activity and morality in a meaningful way. Rather than separating the inquiry into virtue from human life as it is really lived, Aristotle presents his moral theory as something we can take with us into the real world, and utilize to our overall benefit. Aristotle's emphasis on practical moral judgment that utilizes a synthesis of reason, the emotions, and the appetites needs to be understood as an alternative to the ethics of pure reason associated with the Enlightenment that we see reflected today with the penchant for developing analytic models and formulaic approaches.

In order to draw these characters and their circumstances into parallel with our own times, at times I offer direct comparisons between ancient and modern scenarios. The intent of these modern vignettes is not academic in any rigorous sense, but I hope they offer an example of how we might do the work of drawing on Greek literature as we encounter the problems of our own age. My intent here is to point out some of the rhymes of history, and to invite the reader to find others as she chooses.

Our technology would have seemed miraculous to the Greeks, and their writings can seem foreign to students merely because of the absence of familiar paradigms of communication and technology. The students that I teach are well aware that they are entering a rapidly changing world, and they know that they cannot afford to become dependent on a technological paradigm that might become obsolete. In such an environment, it is hardly surprising that these students are suspicious of the past. We must help the next generations see that technological paradigms cannot capture our humanism, and that the study of the humanities is critical to developing an understanding of how human beings function and make decisions. I argue in the essays that follow that the adaptability these young people will need to succeed comes from understanding not just how our human world is different from that of the ancients, but how it is the same.

Chapter 1

Greek Humanism and
the Cartesian Revolution

How much of the human being can be described by science? Is there a limit to the effectiveness of applying quantitative analysis to human affairs? These questions bring us to a disciplinary divide between the humanities and the sciences that has taken on the tone of a battle in recent years. The origins of this divide date back to the 17th century, to what we call the Cartesian separation of mind and body, and the resulting conviction that reason can operate in the domain of science 'purely,' without the influence of irrational physical and human factors. This marked a decisive break with the Greek tradition, a break deliberately orchestrated by the Englishman Francis Bacon (1561-1626) and the Frenchman René Descartes (1596-1650), the founders of modern science and the forebears of modern philosophy.

The Cartesian conviction that reason can free itself from the influence of irrational factors results in the reduction of the essential self to the awareness of oneself as a thinking thing. Descartes's famous statement: "I think, therefore I am," captures this reduction of the self to pure reason. Such a reduction would have been inconceivable to the Greeks, as they embraced the human being in its totality. Recall the famous chorus from Sophocles' *Antigone* that begins: "Many the wonders but nothing is stranger than man," which captures the Greek fascination with the human being and his and her remarkable achievements.[1] For the Greeks, the soul was what animated the body, and this soul included the passions and appetites, as well as our reason. Today's academic emphasis on technical reason, which acknowledges only quantitative processes and results, is a consequence of this decisive turn away from the holistic human organism that so absorbed the Greeks. This modern development, associated with widespread access to technology, returns us to the paradigms of a scientific revolution that took place in the 16th and 17th centuries, about 100 years before the Enlightenment. This paradigm was introduced by Bacon and Descartes. These two men were responsible, almost singlehandedly, for turning the focus of reason away from the contemplative traditions of the Greeks and Christian fathers, and toward the development of scientific processes that could proceed mechanically (impersonally and inevitably) toward a better physical quality of life for all of humanity.

The hard sciences were the primary recipients of this overhaul, but many new scientific disciplines owe their genesis to this shift. The social sciences are relatively new disciplines organized around the principles of quantification that characterized this new tradition. These new sciences worked to bring quantitative scientific tools to problems of human affairs. With all these new social and political problems suddenly offered up to reason to solve, philosophers gained confidence in the primacy of pure reason, a process that would culminate in the radical new teachings about the self-suffi-

---

1   Sophocles. 2013. *Antigone*. In *Antigone, Oedipus the King, Oedipus at Colonus.* Edited by David Grene and Richmond Lattimore. Translated by Elizabeth Wyckoff. Chicago: University of Chicago Press, 33-34.

ciency of reason offered by Immanuel Kant and others in the 18th and 19th centuries.

The notion that the 'human' factor could be removed, and would need to be removed, in order to ensure a scientific outcome was a radical and central component of the work of both Bacon and Descartes. A look back at their insistence on this point offers an interesting perspective on the persistent dualism that separates the sciences and the humanities today. Science and art are long-standing rivals in American universities. The legacy of Baconian and Cartesian science has shaped the way rational and irrational processes have been opposed in our culture, with technical reason on one side, and all human variables on the other.

In this chapter, we will look at the terms of what is called the Cartesian Revolution, so that Greek humanism can emerge in subsequent chapters in contrast. My reasoning here is that we must learn *why* we need to return to the Greeks, and why we are so far from their world-view today, in order to learn the right lessons from their notion of human being.[2]

At first glance, Bacon's contributions to the development of modern experimental sciences do not appear at odds with the idea that individuals may possess some inexplicable combination of qualities that gives them the ability to assess complex situations all at once, and use their intuition, insight, and imagination to guide them to success. Bacon's new scientific method begins with a commitment to work with whatever phenomena present themselves,

---

2   See Krüger, Gerhard. 2007. "The Origin of Philosophical Self-Consciousness." In *The New Yearbook for Phenomenology and Phenomenological Philosophy* Volume 7, 200-259, for a treatment of Descartes' radical break with the Greek tradition.

and is thus centrally concerned with actual conditions. Deduction, by contrast, the method of ancient Greek science, begins with a group of assumptions (that the earth orbits around the sun, for example, or that God set the planets to orbit in perfect circles) and reasons out their consequences. Deduction works well in theoretical disciplines such as geometry, whose static axioms are admittedly the products of reason. Deduction doesn't work so well when applied to problems involving real world forces, whose solutions rest not on axioms, but on the real properties of changing phenomena.

For these problems, Bacon devised the method of induction. Induction begins with experimentation, to isolate and observe the real properties of the material or process being studied. While the experimenter needs to be attentive to the phenomenon, this attention is not a pure act of contemplation as an end in itself, as it was for Aristotle, but merely a means toward the higher ends of power and dominion. The diversity of nature is not a matter for wonder, but for exploitation, with each unique material having a potential role to play in the design of new machines. For Bacon, experimentation requires a willingness to use force, for "the nature of things betrays itself more readily under the vexations of art than in its natural freedom."[3] After collecting experimental data about the behavior and properties of raw materials, Bacon's scientists will pursue only those hypotheses that are consistent with the data. Induction moves from the particular to the universal, and arrives "last of all" at its laws, and "the most general axioms."[4]

---

3   Bacon, Francis. 1999. *The Great Instauration*. In *Selected Philosophical Works*. Edited by Rose-Mary Sargent. Indianapolis: Hackett Publishing Company, 82.

4   Bacon, Francis. 1999. *New Organon*. In *Selected Philosophical Works*, 92

Bacon's method had a huge impact on the physical sciences. Maxwell's equations (named for the Scottish physicist James Clerk Maxwell, 1831-1879), which form the foundation of electrodynamics, give an example of how the work of English scientist Michael Faraday (1791-1867), who took an inductive approach to the connection between electricity and magnetism, led in just a few years to the complete revision and mathematization of an entire science. Similarly, French chemist Antoine Lavoisier (1743-1794) developed the modern science of chemistry by applying the inductive method to the combinations of gases and liquids.

Bacon's second contribution continued his move away from any focus on the uniqueness of the individual. His second principle was that it was crucial to minimize randomness in the scientific process. Bacon conceived of the experimental process as something that could be mechanized in such a way as to ensure that the scientist exerted no individual influence on the phenomena. In this insistence, Bacon rejected the animistic approach of the ancient Greeks. Bacon describes Aristotle's notion of final cause (the 'essence' of the thing), and Aristotle's other qualitative categories, as "fantastical and ill defined."[5] Bacon rejects quality in favor of quantitative measures.

Bacon did not see himself as building on an older tradition, but as offering a complete rebuilding of human learning. Because of the existing muddle of human knowledge, Bacon considered that "there was but one course left, therefore, to try the whole thing anew upon a better plan, and to commence a total reconstruction of sciences, arts, and all human knowledge raised upon the proper foundation."[6] Bacon was committed to technological

5   Ibid, 91.
6   Bacon, *The Great Instauration*, 66.

advances that would elevate the human condition and contribute to a better quality of life. Bacon advocated seeking the "true ends of knowledge" not for their own sake, as the Greeks had insisted, but "for the benefit and use of life."[7] For Bacon, the foundations of knowledge rest on "human utility and power."[8]

In order to minimize randomness, Bacon replaced the Hellenic notion of the soul as a combination of rational and irrational aspects with a systematic mental apparatus that would give the quest for mastery over nature machine-like properties. The first item of business was to identify and remove the human predilections and prejudices that hold reason back from its methodical attainment of certainty. For Bacon, these prejudices fall into four classes of what he calls "Idols," in an attempt to shock his readers into acknowledging that the adherence to the existing edifice of assumptions was a matter of faith, not reason. Bacon's four classes of Idols are organized around four fundamental types of scientific errors to which the human mind is susceptible. These errors have to do with 1) mistaken perceptions; 2) biases stemming out of the mental and bodily constitution of the individual, such as her education, her habits, and the accidents that have composed her experience; 3) hidden propensities that stem from relying on existing terms and their definitions; and 4) dogmatism arising out of false adherence to received systems of thought. Once the idols are exposed and banished, Bacon argued, the method should be foolproof. The scientist will be objective, his or her preconceptions and biases held to be of no account. All an individual would need to attain objectivity was to adopt this methodology. Ironically, this Baconian syllogism

7   Ibid, 75.

8   Ibid.

could quickly turn into an idol of its own. This 'faith' in objectivity attained by adopting the scientific method was soon to be affirmed by René Descartes with decisive results.

The widespread adoption of the Baconian commitment to the certainty of an objective result might not have been so inevitable had it not been for the work of this French philosopher. Born 35 years after Francis Bacon, Descartes did for philosophy, the study of ends, what Bacon did for natural science. While Bacon rejected the existing corpus of knowledge about the natural world, Descartes performed a similar overhaul of the basic premises of ontology, the study of being. In his *Discourse on the Method*, Descartes documents the results of his own philosophical experiment with a methodology of radical doubt in terms that are reminiscent of Bacon's own radical understanding of his proposed method. "I formed a method," Descartes reports in 1637, "whereby I can increase my knowledge gradually."[9]

Descartes' philosophical certainty is based on a series of rules, analogous to the stages in Bacon's infallible "machinery." The rules begin with Descartes' resolve to "never accept anything as true if I did not have evident knowledge of its truth," and continue with a reductive, analytical method that will "divide each difficulty into as many parts as possible in order to resolve them better," and, finally, to "direct my thoughts in an orderly manner... and ascend from simplest to most complex."[10] The paradigm shift that Descartes' radical doubt represents for the type of authority we now look to

---

9   Descartes, René. 1985. *Discourse on the Method*. in *The Philosophical Writings of Descartes*. Translated by Cottingham, Stoothoff, and Murdoch. Cambridge: Cambridge University Press, 112.

10   Ibid, 120.

for truth can hardly be overstated. Descartes' "evident knowledge" was not the self-evident fact of his existence that the Greeks would have assumed. In his radical doubt, Descartes entertains even the possibility that he is being deceived about his sensory experience by a malevolent deity. Hence "evident knowledge" refers here only to those pure processes of reason that have been scrupulously inspected for logical fallacy.

Apart from these programmatic similarities, Bacon and Descartes have very little in common. While Descartes' approach begins with an 'experiment' of sorts, intended to reveal the prop-erties of the subject's own thought-process itself, the experiment begins not with the sensory particulars, as Bacon advocated, but with an attempt to isolate the mind from all effects of sense percep-tion. "Because our senses sometimes deceive us," Descartes explains, "I decided to suppose that nothing was such as they led us to imag-ine."[11] Descartes describes his thought-experiment as a meditation, stressing that it had to be done alone, by an individual in isolation rather than in collaboration with others. For Descartes, skepticism was an individual tool, one that only a passionate lover of wisdom would undertake.

Descartes was struck that, although he could doubt the reality of his body, he could not doubt the reality of his mind. The funda-mental premise "I am thinking, therefore I exist," Descartes writes, is the "only thing that I can't doubt."[12] This led Descartes to posit that mind and body were different substances. Descartes proceeds deductively from his conviction that his thought-process was the only thing he could be certain was real. This premise, known by its

11   Ibid, 127.
12   Ibid.

Latin phrasing *cogito ergo sum*, led Descartes to his famous conclusion that mind and body are entirely separate. "This 'I' – the soul by which I am what I am," Descartes continues, "is entirely distinct from the body."[13]

With this conclusion, Descartes separated being into two categories: *Res cogitans* (the stuff of mind) and *res extensa* (the stuff of nature). Instead of being interconnected with what is 'out there,' the human mind was now declared independent and internal, not of the natural world, but altogether separated from it. Descartes himself may not have meant this separation to be taken literally, for he presents his conclusion here as "a fable," because he is aware that the "charm of fables awakens the mind."[14] Regardless, the Cartesian separation of mind and nature is still taken by many sciences as axiomatic. This dogmatic reception overlooked many of the problems with Descartes' thought-experiment, and dismissed any evidence that human reason might be more 'contaminated' by nature than the Cartesian premise allowed. As the Enlightenment sceptic Voltaire would put it one hundred years later, Descartes was "born to bring to light the errors of antiquity and to put his own in their place."[15] Despite its questionable status, this dualism took hold as Descartes' greatest legacy: "Descartes left as one of his main philosophical legacies a myth," namely the assumption that the object of science was something inherently separated from the inquiring scientist.[16]

---

13 Ibid.
14 Ibid, 112.
15 Voltaire. 1961. *Philosophical Letters*, Translated by Ernest Delworth. Indianapolis: Bobbs-Merrill Company, 53.
16 Ryle, Gilbert. 2000. *The Concept of Mind*. Chicago: University of Chicago Press, 8.

Regardless of its author's intent, the Cartesian separation of mind and body was taken as confirmation of the viability of Bacon's vision of a 'pure', scientific objectivity. If the mind is altogether different from all other phenomena, it can hold itself apart as the observer, without having any effect on the matter under observation. The adoption of this dualistic assumption provided scientists with the self-confidence to go through with the complete rejection of inherited doctrine.[17] Cartesian dualism has influenced the scientific method by bolstering the scientist's belief in his own isolation from the phenomena. Reason, or so goes the Cartesian myth, can affirm the validity of its own processes by withdrawing completely from the extended world.

Descartes outlines his famous thought-experiment in a 1637 text, *Discourse on the Method of Rightly Conducting One's Reason and of Seeking Truth in the Sciences*, whose title draws attention to Descartes' belief that his separation of mind from body would have profound implications for science. As an appendix to this work, Descartes attached his *Geometry*, in which he outlines his new method of analytic geometry. Descartes intended this new method to "take over all that is best in geometrical analysis and in algebra, using the one to correct all the defects of the latter."[18] Descartes linked this new mathematics to his conviction that God's plan for nature is mirrored in the abstract processes of reason that constitute the unique substance of mind. In this view, understanding nature requires not extending ourselves more consciously into its phenomena, but withdrawing inward and applying abstract

---

17   See Valery, Paul. 1978. "Une vue de Descartes," *Variete V*. Paris: Site Gallimard, 218.
18   Descartes, *The Philosophical Writings*, 121.

processes of reason: "I have noticed certain laws which God has so established in nature, and of which he has implanted such notions in our minds, that after adequate reflection we cannot doubt that they are exactly observed in everything which exists or occurs in the world."[19]

Descartes' rules for certitude require extensive modeling. The primary modeling tool of the *Geometry* is the Cartesian coordinate system. The coordinate system enabled Descartes to reduce phenomena to geometric shapes and then map these shapes onto a numerical system. Descartes explains reduction and numerization as necessary steps on the way to "perfect" understanding: "If we perfectly understand a problem we must abstract it from every superfluous conception, reduce it to its simplest terms, and, by means of an enumeration, divide it up into the smallest possible parts."[20] The coordinate system provides the basis for Cartesian systems analysis, and enables such analysis to solve problems of probability and prediction.

Cartesian systems analysis presumes that the analyst maintains a 'God's eye' view from a vantage point outside or above the coordinate system. This perspective was also the assumption of Euclidean geometry, although for Euclid this perspective was understood as an abstraction, not something that one could 'really' obtain. Descartes' dualistic view of mind as something separate from nature enables him to elevate this perspective to that of a real insight that the mind can obtain into the mathematical laws of nature.

---

19   Ibid, 131.
20   Descartes, *Rules for the Direction of the Mind*. In *The Philosophical Writings*, 51.

From the beginning, Baconian science and Cartesian systems analysis were associated with war. Francis Bacon identified the three greatest inventions of all time as printing, gunpowder, and the magnet, essentially the tools of European expansion. Gunpowder provided the war technology, printing enabled mass communications, and the magnet enabled the navigation of men and weapons across great distances. The rising influence of the sciences was the result of European success at waging war. Bacon was not apologetic; he linked humanity's best interests to the design of technology that could direct vast amounts of force toward humankind's chosen ends. Humankind's most glorious accomplishment, according to Bacon, would be to harness nature's powers and control nature's forces, an accomplishment that would ensure "the power and dominion of the human race itself over the universe."[21] Bacon's vision for new technologies that could manage force on a grand scale inclined him to link his ideas about human progress to the rhetoric of power and dominion.

In making an explicit connection between warfare and improvement in the human condition, Bacon stresses the importance of developing new war technology. This is because of the link between success in war and impetus for research. As Bacon notes of history, "the same times that are most renowned for arms are likewise most admired for learning."[22] However, Bacon intended the learning that would characterize the new age to be governed by his own rigorous standards, rather than the looser, contemplative traditions of the Greeks. This aspect of Bacon's work undermined any notion that the mechanistic approach of the modern sciences could be compatible

---

21 Bacon, *New Organon*, 129.
22 Bacon, *Selected Philosophical Works*, 10.

with the older humanist tradition, with its focus on the individual as a being in whom the rational and irrational are entwined. Bacon insisted, as did Descartes, that irrational, 'human' variables could and should be entirely removed from the scientific process.

Warfare for the moderns means improved technology that will raise our physical quality of living. Yet quality of living is not a philosophical improvement in our condition, but merely a material one. The relentlessly utilitarian emphasis on improved quality of living has not helped us understand any better what it means to be a human being. In later chapters, I hope to show that for the Greeks, it was just the opposite. In each of the major wars that they fought up until the 4th century BCE: the Trojan War, the Persian Wars, and the Peloponnesian War, the Greeks discovered something essential about their way of being human.

Bacon's utilitarian humanism, by contrast to Greek humanism, is based on a notion of human rights that prioritizes giving everyone access the same material conditions of life. If human beings are inherently equal, they are equally deserving of improvement in their quality of life. The only way to offer such improvements to all of humankind is to implement technology on a grand scale. While this goal is humanitarian, its means are mechanical and inhuman. Bacon insisted that personal factors must not influence the outcome of scientific investigation, which should consist of mechanistic methods that could be replicated by any scientist without alteration.[23] If a discipline was to offer tangible universal benefit, it would have to be through the establishment of fool-proof axioms that could be used as the basis for quantifiable determinations of real-world conditions.

---

23 Bacon, *Selected Philosophical Works*, xxiv-xxv.

The Cartesian Revolution had a huge influence on how problems of leadership and strategy would be approached. In what follows, I hope to show that the Greek definition of humanism is also important from the perspective of effective decision-making. The ancient Greek historian Herodotus tells a story about Phidippides, who was running the first 'marathon' from Athens to Sparta to report the Persian invasion when the god Pan called out to him. When he told the story in Athens, the Athenians rushed to build a shrine and offer sacrifices to Pan. The Athenians were rational but not secular – they didn't strenuously separate religion from politics, nor did they find this interactivity with their gods incompatible with their pursuit of rational political theory. The Athenians, who loved art and sports, who produced great works of literature and philosophy, saw no contradiction in living in a world also habited by gods, spirits, and souls.

Referring to this story, Robert Kaplan argues that the strict segregation of rational and irrational, science and spirit, might lead our imaginations to fail us in critical ways: "If rationalism and secularism have taken us so far that we can no longer imagine what Phidippides saw, then we are incapable of understanding – and consequently defending ourselves against – many of the religious movements that reverse the Enlightenment and affect today's geopolitics."[24] Alongside any failure to understand our enemies, in our inability to understand the ancient Greeks, whose heritage we also draw on, we are failing to understand ourselves.

Rationalism and secularism together oppose the role of the irrational in human affairs, a role that Greek authors as diverse as

24 Kaplan, Robert. 2007. "A Historian for Our Time." *The Atlantic*, Jan/Feb 2007. https://www.theatlantic.com/magazine/archive/2007/01/a-historian-for-our-time/305562/

Plato and Thucydides took seriously. In light of recent evidence for the profound influence of irrational factors on human economic, political, and social choice, it is all the more important to understand the way our secular rationalism puts us at odds with the Greeks.[25] The mutual exclusivity of the domains of the rational and irrational has been challenged scientifically by the field of neuropsychology, and philosophically by phenomenology. Yet the growing authority of technical reason in academic affairs returns us to the definitive break with the Greek way of being in the world that was engineered by Bacon and Descartes. The Baconian and Cartesian projects rejected any sense of their animated interconnectivity with the natural world, and established in its place mechanical, foolproof methodologies based on a notion of the scientist as someone isolated and detached from natural phenomena, someone who could manipulate the physical world without being influenced in return. This radical rejection of the Hellenic interactivity between human beings and the world they lived in set the stage for the culture clash that concerns Kaplan, the clash between rationalism and animism that makes it so difficult for Westerners to imagine the world-views of Hindu culture, and the folk cultures of North Africa and Indonesia, among others.

America's relationship with science and technology differs from Europe's, for America was founded just as the Baconian and Cartesian revolutions were gaining traction. Just as young children master new technology more quickly than those who must give up old

---

25 See Kaplan, Robert. 2002. *Warrior Politics: Why Leadership Demands a Pagan Ethos.* New York: Vintage Books. The TEDx library offers a good sampling of recent research on the role on the irrational in economic, social and political behavior.

ways in order to embrace the new, America absorbed the framework of the Cartesian revolution during the country's infancy. The methods of induction and systems analysis dominated the defense industry from its inception. Defense technology has in turn shaped academic progress in America in an unusual way, pitting engineering against the human-based understanding of the importance of individual intellectual curiosity. In 1961, President Eisenhower warned of the dangers of allowing the technological mindset of the defense industry to dominate our institutions of higher learning: "our arms must be mighty, ready for instant action," and yet the domestic defense industry that maintains our armament threatens to make "the free university" into the "captive of a scientific-technological elite."[26] In America, Cartesian systems analysis has formed the basis for our technological dominance, and tends to be self-perpetuating by the diverting of academic resources toward research that utilizes the Cartesian premise. Cartesian systems analysis is a powerful academic authority, not just in the hard sciences, but in the social sciences as well.

Yet the bifurcation between science and the human being remains apparent. Big technology, grounded in Baconian induction and Cartesian systems analysis, has not stopped terrorism, nor has it helped us work closely and develop trusting relationships with people whose values and world-views are very different from our own.[27] Although defense technology is developed in accordance with the Baconian inductive method, and kinetic warfare is

---

26 Eisenhower, Dwight. "Farewell Address." 17 January, 1961. https://www. ourdocuments.gov/doc.php?flash=false&doc=90&page=transcript

27 See, for example, Kilcullen, David. 2006. "Twenty-Eight Articles," *Small Wars Journal*, summer 2006, article 13, (Build Trusted Networks). smallwarsjournal.com/documents/28 articles.pdf.

implemented through a method that follows Bacon in attempting to eliminate all human variables, the military mission continues to depend on human-to-human encounters that can bridge cultural differences. There is now a steady call from within the ranks for military leadership "that understands the present," and can plan for military contexts that are "not merely in artillery shells and Tomahawk missiles," but require "broad interaction with people not like us."[28]

Despite Bacon's hope for universal improvement to the quality of human life, Third World cultures missed out on the subsequent Enlightenment, and continue to understand the world through deductions from what the West views as primitive hypotheses. The challenges of interacting with these cultures can profit from a better understanding of how American rationalism and secularism have tended to limit the domain of reason to those technical processes that do not depend on human variability.

Rationalism holds that truth is not accessible to the senses, but only to the mind. The political view that the human is an inherently self-interested, reasonable, and independent being was shaped by Enlightenment thinkers such as John Locke (1632-1704), David Hume (1711-1776), and Charles, Baron of Montesquieu (1689-1755). Advocates of this view in America included Thomas Jefferson (1743-1826) and Benjamin Franklin (1706-1790).[29] Political science and

---

28 Kohllmann, Benjamin. 2012. "The Military Needs More Disruptive Thinkers." *Small Wars Journal*, 5 April 2012. Web.

29 For an overview, see Anchor, Robert. 1967. *The Enlightenment Tradition*. Berkeley: University of California Press. In America, founders Hamilton and Madison argued the opposite view that the individual is ruled by irrational passions. Hamilton, Alexander, Jay, John, and James Madison. 2001. *The Federalist*. Edited by George W. Carey and James McClellan. Carmel: Liberty Fund Books.

economics developed on the premise that the individual is a rational actor who will calculate his actions based on his or her material and physical self-interest. The British philosopher John Stuart Mill (1806-1873) posited further that this rational actor makes ethical decisions according to principles of utilitarianism, principles that provide a quantitative, reductive formula for determining the course that will maximize pleasure and minimize pain.

The popular rational-actor theory model has its empirical foundations in the work of Bacon and Descartes, who introduced the quantitative methods of reductionism, methods that isolate phenomena and describe phenomena in mathematical terms. In making science synonymous with mechanical analysis, Bacon and Descartes accomplished their self-professed task of rejecting the doctrines of science inherited from the Greeks and passed down through the Middle Ages. Through their work, Bacon and Descartes changed not just science, but our basic notions about how we come to know the world and how we exist in it. Bacon envisioned a method of induction that would function mechanistically, having eliminated the influence of all irrational factors. Descartes' radical separation of mind and body introduced the concept of reason as something autonomous, separate from its environment, that could with confidence bring its detached processes to bear on philosophical, mathematical, and physical problems, provided it followed certain prescribed methods of deductive analysis. This new view of science as a set of mechanical processes came to characterize the different scientific disciplines, and allowed advocates to assert their discipline as distinct from all others, each now with a unique domain and an independent set of variables. Thanks to Descartes, each discipline could now plug its variables into standard mathematical formulae and study its phenomena quantitatively using Cartesian systems analysis. The new social sciences of management, leadership, and military studies adopted these methods.

Given the relationship between Baconian science and Europe's military success, it is striking that warfare itself has remained resistant to the terms of the Baconian scientific method. The difficulties in reducing warfare to a technical science illustrate the problem with surrendering too quickly the Greek humanist focus on the role of irrational human factors to the narrower terms of technical reason. Antoine-Henri Jomini (1779-1869) attempted to provide a scientific framework for warfare, in his *Treatise on Grand Tactics*. Long a staple at the U.S. Military Academy, Jomini's attempt to turn strategy into science fell out of favor after the Civil War illustrated the limitations of this approach.[30]

The limitations of the technical, mechanistic approach are apparent in many disciplines today, including strategic studies, which is concerned with the qualities of leadership that will preserve and extend America's power in world affairs. In the mid-1800's, West Point was training its officers in Jomini's technical war manual, yet the Civil War undermined Jomini's scientific hypotheses, and showed the importance of irrational factors like intuition and heart to the waging of a successful campaign.

To illustrate the failures of Jomin's purported science of war, it is useful to consider the relative examples of the Civil War generals George McClellan (1826-1885) and William Tecumseh Sherman (1820-1894). While both excelled at West Point, even there the

---

30 See McPherson, James. 1997. *For Cause and Comrades: Why Men Fought in the Civil War*. Oxford: Oxford University Press.

difference between them was apparent. McClellan, second in the class of 1846, was attracted to Jomini's theoretical approach to the art of war. McClellan was a by-the-book strategist who had demonstrated his mastery of big war science. McClellan excelled at training and organizing armies, but in the field, his calculations paralyzed him, and he was unable to translate his theoretical knowledge into real-world military success. McClellan was eventually relieved of command by President Lincoln, who offered a diplomatic assessment of how McClellan could be so knowledgeable in theory and yet so incapable in real life combat: "If he can't fight himself, he excels in making others ready to fight.[31]

To history, McClellan's hesitancy caricatures the deficiency of the mechanical view when taken alone, without a corresponding intuition for battle. McClellan's antithesis, Sherman, had both. Sherman excelled at operations and maintaining discipline, but in both his capture of Atlanta and his famous "March to the Sea" in 1864, he followed a renegade strategy of total war that relied heavily on his own intuitive design. Sixth in his class at West Point, Sherman writes of his time there that, "I was not considered a good soldier, for at no time was I selected for any office, but remained a private throughout the whole four years. Then, as now, neatness in dress and form, with a strict conformity to the rules, were the qualifications for office, and I suppose I was found not to excel in any of these."[32] Caring more about the 'soul' of battle than its external form, Sher-

---

31 McPherson, James. 2008. *Tried by War: Abraham Lincoln as Commander in Chief.* London: Penguin Books, 122; see also Godwin, Doris Kearns. 2005. *Team of Rivals: The Political Genius of Abraham Lincoln.* New York: Simon and Schuster.

32 Sherman, William. 2013. *Memoirs of General W. T. Sherman.* CreateSpace Independent Publishing Platform,, 12.

man studied broadly across the humanities and sciences: "Education rather than purely military education was critical in Sherman's view, and it ranged from art and literature to language and science, always to be tested and refined by the firsthand knowledge of the "man of action.""[33] Sherman helped the North win victory with his decisive march through the South, a march that was a "hard species of war," and yet also "more statesmanship than war" in its minimal infliction of casualties and unorthodox avoidance of the big war techniques that preoccupied McClellan.[34]

There are many other examples of how Cartesian systems analysis becomes problematic when applied to systems of phenomena that are inherently unstable. Defense technology has only partially addressed the problem of war's unpredictability. Despite a historical association between military conquest and leisure, warfare itself has resisted attempts to reduce it to a science. After Jomini's scientific manual of strategy fell out of favor after the Civil War, the Prussian general and military thinker Carl von Clausewitz (1780-1831) became the favored author of strategic theory. In his manual, *On War*, Clausewitz approached strategy in the spirit of the Greek humanist tradition, by acknowledging the role of reason and the irrational alike. Clausewitz combines Cartesian methods with a deep respect for complex, irrational factors within individual agents and within the circumstances. Clausewitz advocated an approach that balanced technical aspects of war with an emphasis on the critical role in real world scenarios of individual human judgment.

---

33 Hanson, Victor Davis. 1999. *The Soul of Battle*. New York: Simon and Schuster, 216.
34 Ibid,149.

Clausewitz addressed the question of whether war is an art or a science in a chapter of his treatise entitled "Art or Science of War." This chapter begins in the manner of an Aristotelian treatise, relying on definition of terms to establish which category is more apt. "We have already said elsewhere that 'knowing' is something different from 'doing,'" Clausewitz writes, in classic Aristotelian style.[35] Science involves knowing, and Clausewitz acknowledges that the successful commander must have knowledge. Yet this knowledge must be converted into action that results in victory, and this conversion, Clausewitz argues, can occur only in a mind that is at home amongst an ever-shifting environment. Clausewitz makes this distinction the basis for his rejection of the view that warfare could be a science.

> If the architect takes up a pen to settle the strength of a pier by a complicated calculation, the truth found as a result is no emanation from his own mind. He had first to find the data with labour, and then to submit these to an operation of the mind, the rule for which he did not discover. But it is never so in War. The moral reaction, the ever-changeful form of things, makes it necessary for the chief actor to carry in himself the whole mental apparatus of his knowledge, that anywhere and at every pulse-beat he may be capable of giving the requisite decision from himself (II, II).

War cannot be science, Clausewitz argues in the chapter "Art of Science of War," because the forces on which it acts are themselves human in nature:

---

35 von Clausewitz, Carl. 1991. *On War*, Book II, Chapter III. Translated by J. J. Graham. Web.

War is no activity of the will, which exerts itself upon inanimate matter like the mechanical Arts; or upon a living but still passive and yielding subject, like the human mind and the human feelings in the ideal Arts, but against a living and reacting force. (II, II).

Following up on the theme that war operates in the human domain, Clausewitz goes on to dismiss both the labels as inadequate: "We say therefore War belongs not to the province of Arts and Sciences, but to the province of social life" (II, III). Clausewitz' insistence on the primacy of action over theory has made his manual popular reading not just in military and political circles, but in business and finance as well, where his manual is a European alternative to Sun Tzu's *The Art of War*, a manual of decisive leadership for individuals who want to get ahead in any field. Clausewitz's *On War* acknowledges the role of unscientific human qualities such as intuition, emotion, imagination, and spirit. Clausewitz criticizes theoretical approaches to war that "direct the attention only on material forces," the kinetic fight, while disregarding the way "military action is penetrated throughout by moral forces and their effects" (II, II). Clausewitz goes on to urge that in the case of strategic studies, "science must become art," and, "one condition which is more necessary for the knowledge of the conduct of war than for any other, is that it must pass completely into the mind and almost completely cease to be something objective" (II, II). Clausewitz' disregard for the Cartesian duality between subject and object sets up a kinship between his approach and that of the Greeks, who were interested in the way an individual could bring all of his human qualities to bear on a situation.

Other academics have taken seriously Clausewitz' suggestion that we discard the duality between science and art, because it is a stance that is of no value for developing effective strategists. In his 1976 *The Face of Battle*, John Keegan drew attention to the need for war historians to develop pathways that can navigate between the mechanical considerations of armament and operations and the individual's experience. Keegan finds good reasons for military academies to offer a "de-sensitized treatment of war," and sees that "the categorical, reductive quality of officer-training has an important and intended – if subordinate – psychological effect," namely by conveying effective tools for managing the stress of actual combat.[36] At the military academies, the nature of the vocational training attempts "to exclude from his field of vision everything that is irrelevant to his professional function, and to define all that he ought to see in a highly formal manner." For cadets' academic studies, however, Keegan finds it important "to offer the student not a single but a variety of angles of vision," which will require the broader approach of the liberal arts.[37] The Clausewitzian ideal is someone like William Tecumseh Sherman, whose conduct of the Union Army's critical march through the South shows that he functioned equally well in the midst of method and mayhem alike.[38]

Keegan's work and Clausewitz's ideals are all the more important now, since the Cartesian gap between pure reason and the irrational has been further narrowed by scientists who see the need for the study of complex, adaptive systems. In mathematics, biology, ecology, artificial intelligence, and the social sciences, Carte-

---

36 Keegan, John. 1976. *The Face of Battle*. London: Penguin Books, 13-20.
37 Ibid, 22-23.
38 Hanson, *The Soul of Battle*, 149.

sian systems analysis is increasingly giving way to post-Cartesian complex systems analysis, which can more successfully be applied to phenomena now understood to behave in nonlinear manner. In recent decades, the rational actor premise has come under criticism for its inability to account for economic and political behavior, and for its failure as a premise of foreign and defense policy.[39] Philosophy too has participated in this shift, with a new school of phenomenological studies. Within the last decade, the military has also drawn on complexity theory to obtain models for a post-Cartesian approach to counterinsurgency.[40]

The Greek humanist tradition has something to offer in this environment. The Greeks lived in an animated world, in which plants, animals, and humans represent a graduated collection of souls. They saw the human as a being in constant interaction with nature, with form shaped for function, and the human, as it were, "tuned for relationship."[41] With so many disciplines now returning to this Hellenic assumption that complex patterns of connectivity and interactivity exist between the human being and his or her environment, we might wonder how the technological revolution might have looked had Bacon and Descartes not insisted that the scientist be disconnected, cut off, and isolated from the influence of his or her sensual environment in order to do science to it. Reductionism has been successful in solving problems of engineering, technology, and operations, thus granting validity to the reductionist assumption that the Aristotelian principle of interconnectivity has no place in any scientific analysis.

---

39 For example, Paul, T. V., Morgan, Patrick and James Wirtz, editors. *Complex Deterrence: Strategy in the Global Age*. Chicago: University of Chicago Press.
40 Kilcullen, "Twenty-Eight Articles," op cit.
41 Abrams, David. 1997. *The Spell of the Sensuous*. New York: Vintage Press, ix.

In serving as the champion of inductive reasoning, Bacon rejected both the dogmatists of his age, who believed the laws of nature were already "searched out and understood" and the skeptics, who believed that nothing could be known.[42] "My object," Bacon announced in 1620, is "to open a new way for the understanding, a way… untried and unknown."[43] Bacon's contemporaries relied on Greek methods, particularly those of Aristotle, whose *Categories* constituted the corpus of received knowledge about ways of classifying being. But Bacon's relationship with the ancient Greeks was adversarial. He advocated the rejection of all received knowledge, and a systematic rebuilding of natural science on the basis of the inductive method.

As the founder of the modern technological vision, Bacon was concerned by the encroachment into science of unscientific, human prejudices, and biases. Regarding deduction, the method of the ancients, Bacon understood its popularity in the natural sciences as the result of the human propensity to leap prematurely to conclusions. "The mind," Bacon cautions, "longs to spring up to positions of higher generality, that it might find rest there."[44] By viewing the mind as something undisciplined and lazy, Bacon is able to install his inductive method as a set of instruments, a 'machinery' that if properly applied, will produce results far more certain than any the wandering, prejudiced mind can come up with on its own.

Greek literature illustrates an altogether different way of coming to terms with the inherent irrationality of the human mind. For the Greeks, the emphasis was not on collective humanity, but on

42 Bacon, *New Organon*, 86

43 Ibid, 88.

44 Ibid, 92.

the individual; not on technological mastery of nature, but of the human embeddedness within the natural world. As we go forward into the 21st century, surely both these paradigms should remain very much alive. In the chapters that follow, I will look at some examples of how this experience of being embeddedness in the world led the Greeks to a robust sense of what it means to be a human being. Interestingly, it was through their experience of war and conflict that the Greeks' self-knowledge was developed. It is this process that we want more fully to understand.

Chapter 2

Honor and Atrocity in Homer's *Iliad*

On the rare black figure pottery from the 8th century BCE, mythological scenes from Homer's *Iliad* are common subjects, particularly scenes of warriors and athletes. Men are depicted in action, caught in freeze-frame in the midst of combat or contest. One vase shows a tight pack of runners, another, two wrestlers with legs interlocked, a third, warriors with spears lifted, or swords at the ready. Clearly, the men of this time expected to spend their lives in motion. While this art is lovely, it is also disturbing. Black figures appear as shadows against a red background. The forms of these males are constructed out of a seeming collection of stock body parts, all triangular in shape. Head, torsos, thighs, and calves are inverted triangles, each tip resting on the base below, so that the parts are held together not by joints but by a single, geometrical point. This haunting art has much to tell us about the Homeric world-view, particularly in its suggestion that a man was not a unity, but a conglomerate of disparate parts. Linguistic evidence supports this as well. The Homeric dialect has no word for the live human body as a whole; there is a word, *nekros*, but it refers only to a corpse. This physical disjointedness extends to the psychological as well. The Homeric dialect also has no word for the human soul; the idea of *psyche* as something that could, and should, be unified would not find expression for many hundreds of years after Homer.

Given what we now know of the body's holistic systems, disjointedness has come to be associated with **trauma**. A limb is not seen as an independent component without some accompanying awareness of the violence it would take to separate it from the rest of the body. Part of the shock of seeing an amputee is the awareness that her body has been subjected to an awful force. In the *Iliad*, the joints are painfully vulnerable. The Homeric warrior could cover the massive centers of each part with armor, yet the joints would be left exposed; many of the strikes described in this narrative are directed at the joints: the groin, the shoulder, the neck, the hip, and the knee. Thus the Homeric warrior lived with the constant threat of disintegration, a threat that exposes the fragility of the ties that bound his parts into a living whole. Such is the world of Homer's *Iliad*, a world of force that rips men apart, critiqued bitterly by the French philosopher, Simone Weil, in her essay "The *Iliad*, Poem of Might," written in 1939 on the eve of another age of warfare.[1]

The Homeric hero is destined for pain and trauma; indeed, the very terms by which he could earn status as a hero necessitated trauma. These are the terms of the Homeric hero cult, the folk religion that dictated that a warrior who wished to make a name for himself must seek out a death in battle that will leave his comrades grief-stricken over his corpse.[2] Heroic fame was associated with the willingness to direct oneself toward a death that would be cata-

[1] Weil, Simone. 1965. "The Iliad, or the Poem of Force." *Chicago Review*, 18.2: 5-30.

[2] In the Homeric hero cult, the warrior had to die in order to achieve full honors as a hero. See Volk, Katherina. 2002. "Kleos Aphthitos Revisited." *Classical Philology* 97.1: 61-68.

strophic for his survivors. The psychological cruelty of these terms, which ask the warrior to oppose his love of honor to all his human loves, makes the Homeric hero cult unsustainable; not surprisingly, no new cult sites appear to have been added after the Bronze Age that Homer describes.

In the *Iliad*, this voluntary tearing apart of the emotions that was set as a requisite for heroic honor affects Achaean (Greek) warriors more than Trojan, for the Trojans are for the most part all brothers, fighting not for heroic honor but for defense of wives, sisters, parents, and children. Trojan morale is sustained by the ongoing need to ward off death and destruction from family and home. The Achaeans, by contrast, have said goodbye to their families in order to travel overseas and join a coalition of warriors who live together in a tent city. The bonds that connect the Achaean army are the military bonds of comradeship. Apart from Hector's heartbreaking rejection in Book Six of Andromache's plea that he focus on defending the weak spot in the Trojan walls rather than march out to more offensive terrain, we don't see the Trojan warriors having to reject intimacy in order to seek out honor in the way the Achaeans have already done – and in particular, of course, the Achaean hero, Achilles.

In Achilles' case, a famous prophecy has forced him to commit himself to his choice of a heroic death over a life with his intimates even before sailing for Troy. Once at Troy, the circumstances of Achilles' quarrel with Agamemnon force Achilles to go through this choice a second time, this time with respect to his intimacy with his beloved comrade and foster brother, Patroclus. In what follows, we will look at how Achilles struggles with his choice on this second occasion, in order to understand how Achilles is shattered when the conflict between his honor and his love for Patroclus come into crisis. When his beloved comrade dies, Achilles' grief, pain, and rage lead him to acts of violence that we label atrocities, acts that include berserk killing, reprisal killing, cold-blooded killing of non-combatants, and the mutilation of the corpse.

In the Achaean army, comradeship constitutes an ethical bond between elite warriors of different tribes. A warrior's obligations to his military comrades include mutual defense, the bolstering of each other's spirit for the fight, and recovery of the dead, all of which have a central role in the *esprit de corps* that develops in troop units today. In the *Iliad*, however, comrades routinely engage in one other behavior that the Law of Armed Conflict now forbids: revenge killings to avenge one's fallen comrades. The Law of Armed Conflict is the product of the Enlightenment, and distinguishes the rationalist, moral code of the profession of arms from tribal codes based on revenge and retaliation. Yet many have pointed out recently that this distinction is based on the assumption that the soldier fights for abstract causes like country or ideology, which have little to do with the way soldiers actually speak of combat as a fight undertaken for the cause of comrades.[3] This ongoing tension between a law based on reason and a soldier's actual emotional response to the loss of a comrade comes to our attention frequently now that a 24-hour digital media can instantly turn an atrocity linked to revenge into a global scandal. Reprisal killing has been identified as a motive in

---

3   See Sherman, Nancy. 2010. *The Untold War: Inside the Hearts, Minds, and Souls of our Soldiers.* New York: W. W. Norton & Company, 66; McPherson, *For Cause and Comrades*; Gray, J. Glenn. 1998. *The Warriors, Reflections on Men in Battle*. Lincoln: Bison Books.

many U.S. atrocity scandals, including My Lai in 1968 and Haditha in 2005. From these reports, we might conclude that comradeship continues today very much as it did in Homeric times, as a relationship that can lead either to the most honorable or to the most savage conduct. Modern authors have suggested that the instinct for revenge may be inseparable from a soldier's solidarity with his comrades, it may come along with more noble comradely conduct as part of what we might call a "package deal."[4]

The American philosopher and WWII army officer J. Glenn Gray (1913-1977) describes the feeling of comradeship as "the essence of fighting morale," and traces it to "the feeling of belonging together" that enables men in battle to share the "boundless capacity for self-sacrifice" that makes war so intoxicating.[5] The ideals of comradeship are fundamental to the organization of the U.S. armed forces, and were glorified even in antiquity, as, for example, in the 5th century BCE historian Herodotus' depiction of the Spartan stand at Thermopylae, still active in the popular imagination, as the 2007 Hollywood blockbuster *300* attests. In Plato's *Symposium*, Phaedrus eulogizes the Sacred Band of Thebes, an army composed of 150 pairs of lovers, who showed that "if there were only some way of contriving that a state or an army should be made up of lovers…, when fighting at each other's side, although a mere handful, they would overcome the world" (178e).[6] Phaedrus' speech in the *Symposium*, as well as fragments from Aeschylus' lost play, *The Myrmidons*, glorifies Achilles' love for Patroclus as the very symbol of the heroic poten-

---

4   Sherman, *The Untold War*, 66.

5   Gray, *The Warriors*, 38-51.

6   Plato. 1961. *Symposium*. In *The Collected Dialogues of Plato*. Translated by Michael Joyce. Edited by Edith Hamilton and Huntington Cairns. Princeton: Princeton University Press, 533.

tial of comradeship. Homer's *Iliad* abounds with warriors who are both willing and eager to risk their lives to come to one another's defense and recover the bodies of their fallen comrades.

Yet even while it supports the goals of combat, comradeship can also be destructive. If a warrior feels he has let his comrades down, the guilt and shame may be overwhelming. If he loses a close comrade, he will suffer grief and rage, those runaway emotions that cannot always be stopped.[7] Achilles' experience encompasses the most intense of these comradely responses. After being stripped of rank (*time* in Greek) for no other reason than that his commander has had to relinquish rank of his own, Achilles persists in his withdrawal from the fighting to the point that his former comrades Ajax and Diomedes view him as a traitor, and his refusal to fight leads directly to the death of his beloved comrade Patroclus.

The destructive instinct that erupts in Achilles after the death of Patroclus characterizes comradeship's darker side, the side that kept J. Glenn Gray from endorsing this relationship wholeheartedly as a moral aspect of warfare. While Gray acknowledges that "the communal experience we call comradeship, is thought… to be especially moral and the one genuine advantage of battle that peace can seldom offer," Gray's own analysis leaves him with some reservations. "Whether this is true or not," he continues, "deserves to be investigated."[8] Those who think comradeship especially moral may be seduced by its idealized aspect and by its glorified portrayals in popular and military culture. Those whose spirits are stirred by the displays of loyalty and self-sacrifice for comrades as depicted in the 2001 film *Black Hawk Down*, for example, might be disillusioned to

7   Sherman, *The Untold War*, 69.
8   Gray, *The Warriors*, 39.

learn that the career of one young captain decorated for this mission ended in disgrace, at the rank of colonel, for condoning his men's reprisal killings in the Iraq War.[9] Achilles' story is far from unique, and suggests that nobility and savagery are not exclusive options, one in accord with, and the other in violation of, some moral rule, but rather successive states that naturally accompany the potential and actual loss of a comrade in combat.

Let us now turn to the textual evidence. As mentioned, Homer's *Iliad* builds the conflict between honor and intimacy into the fundamental terms of Achaean warfare, in that the hero must pursue an elusive honor that can only be earned by inflicting the calamity of his death on those who love him. For Achilles, this irony at the heart of the warrior brotherhood sustains both his most noble emotions and his fiercest, most savage rage.

The protagonist Achilles uniquely personifies this ironic relationship between honor and loss: the very name 'Achilles' is a Greek compound that means "grief to his people."[10] The classicist Gregory Nagy points out that "the figure of Achilles is pervasively associated with the theme of grief."[11] The linkage, in the *Iliad*, of a hero's honor and his survivors' grief led the Homeric scholar James Redfield to call the *Iliad* a "dramatic lament" or "narrative mourning for the defeated hero."[12] The hero cult, formed around self-sacrifice, makes an additional demand on Achilles, who must make the self-sacrifice himself but first witness it in Patroclus, and thus himself undergo

---

9   See Cloud, David and Greg Jaffe. 2010. *The Fourth Star: Four Generals and the Epic Struggle for the Future of the United States Army*. New York: Broadway Books, for the story of Colonel Michael Steele's reprimand.

10 Nagy, Gregory. 1979. *The Best of the Achaeans*. Baltimore: The Johns Hopkins University Press, 69.

11 Ibid, 77.

12 Ibid, "Forward" by James Redfield, X.

the extreme grief that would conventionally be displaced onto his own mourners.

This interrelationship between honor and grief drives the plot of the *Iliad*. Amidst a community that views rank as something external, in this case as booty displayed, something analogous to an insignia, Agamemnon takes Briseis from Achilles because he himself has been ritually stripped of his own external honor. As a result of this insult to his manhood and his sense of fair play, Achilles, along with Patroclus, withdraws from combat. Their withdrawal from the fighting where honor is earned puts both men in a limbo of waiting that ends with Patroclus making the request that will take him to his death. In agreeing to Patroclus' request to return to battle dressed in Achilles' armor, Achilles puts an end to a situation that is intolerable for both him and his friend. And yet, Achilles' acquiescence leads directly to Patroclus' death. While Patroclus' death secures his own heroism and frees Achilles to seek the full honor of his own prophesied death, the circumstances in which this death occurs intensify Achilles' grief unbearably. Achilles' involvement in the death of his closest comrade illustrates the fragmentation of the inner world that marks the terms of the hero cult. To Achilles and the reader, the death of Patroclus represents the way the hero is caught up in a self-shattering drive to sacrifice fellowship, intimacy and even life itself to the quest for immortal honor.[13]

Because of the communal importance of the grief ritual that confirms a hero's status, honor is acted out during the hero's lifetime as a set of behaviors that links warriors in combat, and is anticipated as a relationship that even after death will bond one's

---

13 Simone Weil made this irony the basis for her powerful WWII interpretation of the *Iliad*. Op. cit.

survivors to oneself. Patroclus' dying words attest to the concreteness of this relationship. Patroclus is killed at the end Book Sixteen of the *Iliad*, at the climactic two-thirds point in the Twenty-four book epic. I use the passive voice: 'Patroclus is killed', because Patroclus' death occurs in three stages and can't be attributed to a single agent, not even the agency of Hector, his final vanquisher. Patroclus' last words to Hector draw attention to this ambiguity: "Deadly fate in league with Apollo killed me. From the ranks of men, Euphorbus. You came third, and all you could do was finish off my life..." (16. 993-5).[14]

Despite minimizing Hector's responsibility for his death, Patroclus is nonetheless certain that Achilles will seek vengeance from Hector:

> One more thing – take it to heart, I urge you – you too, you won't live long yourself, I swear. Already I see them looming up beside you – death and the strong force of fate, to bring you down at the hands of Aeacus' great royal son... Achilles! (16. 996-1000)

Why should Achilles go after Hector, if Hector was not Patroclus' true killer? Patroclus presents it as inevitable, and perhaps it is. The sequence of grief to rage is a well-documented human response. Reprisal killing as an expression of grief is a central theme in the personal narratives of Vietnam and Iraq War veterans, and does not always need to have a particular target in mind. Recent approaches to healing war trauma emphasize the therapeutic importance of the soldier's constructing his or her own narrative in his or her own

---

14 Homer. 1990. *The Iliad*, Translated by Robert Fagles. New York: Viking Penguin. All translations from the *Iliad* reference this translation.

words. In one such narrative, written from a prison cell where the author was serving a sentence for murder, one Vietnam veteran reflects on the power of this blind, retaliatory rage: "Even now, I cannot fully explain this barbarous equation: I felt pain, rage, and then I wanted to kill someone."[15]

Achilles and Patroclus were more than comrades-in-arms. Patroclus' dying words testify to an intimate connection that began when they were boys growing up together in the house of Peleus. Achilles and Patroclus are not just comrades, they have also been foster-brothers since childhood. This love that extended throughout their peacetime lives will extend beyond death as well. Patroclus returns in Book Twenty-Three as a ghost to request that Achilles arrange for their bones to be buried in a single urn: "together… just as we grew up together" (23. 102). While the epic depicts Achilles as aloof, the depiction of Patroclus focuses on togetherness and intimacy. Throughout Homer's epic, Patroclus is celebrated for his capacity for relationship and intimacy, an unusually deep man whose primary personal characteristic was compassion. Briseis grieves for Patroclus not because he was a great warrior but because he was kind. At his funeral, she says: "So now I mourn your death – I will never stop – you were always kind (19. 355-6).

Patroclus has the type of kindness that characterizes the Good Samaritan parable of Christian lore. In Book Eleven, he meets the wounded warrior Eurypylus when the two men are alone, without witnesses, and Patroclus is hurrying on a mission that is both offi-

---

15 Anderson, Donald.. 2008. "A Boatman's Story." *In When War Becomes Personal: Soldiers' Accounts From the Civil War to Iraq*. Iowa City: University of Iowa Press, 145.

cial and of deep personal significance to him. [16] Although Patroclus is "moved at the sight" of the wounded Eurypulus, at first it seems that he will not stop to give aid: "Impossible. Eurypylus, hero, what shall we do? I am on my way with a message for Achilles, our great man of war – the plan that Nestor, Achaea's watch and ward, urged me to report" (11.1001-4). Despite its being "impossible" Patroclus finds time to render aid. "But I won't neglect you, even so, with such a wound," he tells Eurypylus (11. 1005). Patroclus puts his arm around Eurypylus' waist, helps him back to his shelter and cares for his wound. These are the requirements of the Christian Good Samaritan parable, which emphasizes that help must be offered freely, without witnesses, and despite the need to delay a personally significant and urgent task.

Patroclus' characteristic compassion and his intimate bond with Achilles are both critical factors in Patroclus' request to take Achilles' armor into battle. Although the swapping of armor is done ritually elsewhere in the *Iliad*, this instance entails a merging of Achilles' and Patroclus' personal identities, wherein Patroclus dons the façade of another, and Achilles permits another to occupy his facade. This literal merging of identity is precisely what distinguishes comradeship from friendship in J. Glenn Gray's opinion, for as Gray points out, "Friends do not seek to lose their identity as comrades… do."[17]

Although the merger of identities is no part of friendship in any Aristotelian sense, it does have overtones of the erotic, such as we find in other aspects of Achilles' relationship with Patroclus.

---

16 Cf. Darley, J. M., and C. D. Batson. 1973. ""From Jerusalem to Jericho": A study of Situational and Dispositional Variables in Helping Behavior," *Journal of Personal and Social Psychology* 27: 100-108.

17 Gray, *The Warriors*, 90.

The scene in which Patroclus requests Achilles' armor has erotic overtones that play out in the form of a game of 'cat and mouse'. As he approaches Achilles after caring for Eurypylus, Patroclus is weeping tears of pity for the wounded commanders: "Patroclus reached Achilles, his great commander, and wept warm tears like a dark spring running down some desolate rock face, its shaded currents flowing" (16. 2-4). While Patroclus' pity is unambiguous, Achilles' response reeks of ambivalence:

> And the brilliant runner Achilles saw him coming,
> [was] filled with pity and spoke out winging words:
> Why in tears, Patroclus?
> Like a girl, a baby running after her mother,
> Begging to be picked up, and she tugs her skirts,
> Holding her back as she tries to hurry off – all tears,
> Fawning up at her, till she takes her in her arms…
> That's how you look, Patroclus, streaming live tears (16. 5-12)

Although Achilles is "filled with pity" he mocks Patroclus' tears and tries to shame him into a more stoic response by likening him to a baby girl begging her mother to pick her up. Achilles' mocking acknowledges Patroclus' suffering but belittles it. While such rhetorical shaming is a common technique used by comrades in battle to help each other fight down distracting emotion, Achilles uses it here in the name of his own, individualistic goals. Although Achilles empathizes with his friend's grief, he doesn't appear to have softened in his attitude toward Agamemnon's officers since he rejected their appeals for reconciliation in Book Nine. Instead, Achilles continues with a taunting guessing game about the cause of Patroclus' tears that suggests he savors his façade of pitilessness, in the same spirit with which he sent Patroclus on the mission to find out the identity of the wounded man carried past his camp, where he says: "Son of Menoetius, soldier after my own heart, now I think they will grovel at my knees, our Achaean comrades begging for their lives. The need has reached them – a need too much to bear" (11. 18-20).

Although students frequently use these lines to condemn Achilles for his failure to live up to a set of contemporary moral standards that require altruism, Achilles' immature fantasy of his comrades approaching him in the posture of supplication probably reveals more about his longing to remain connected to this warrior community than about his selfishness. Unable to find a solution on his own, he imagines his comrades breaking of their own accord the barrier imposed by his betrayal of their former camaraderie. Tragically, Achilles' fantasy sets in motion a chain of events that will end with Patroclus' death.

Despite his taunts, Achilles obviously knows the real cause of his friend's grief. Achilles ends his disingenuous guessing game by coming up on his own with the true reason for Patroclus' tears: "weeping over the Argives, are you? Seeing them die against the hollow ships…?" (16. 18-19). Although Achilles would like to maintain his pitiless facade, he empathizes with his friend's distress. The simile of the baby girl suggests further that Achilles also sympathizes with Patroclus, for although it is mocking, it ends with the mother taking the girl in her arms to give comfort. This detail calls attention to the mother's own engagement in her child's emotions, and when applied to Achilles it reveals that Achilles' ambivalence includes some desire to comfort his grieving friend. This whole interaction with Patroclus can be read as Achilles' inadvertent acknowledgement that he continues to share a bond of intimacy with his former Achaean comrades.

Because of his own sympathy, Achilles cannot entirely mock his friend's pity. Prior to Agamemnon's offense against him, Achilles would have felt a similarly unalloyed pity for his wounded Greek comrades; now he reserves his pity only for his loyal friend Patroclus. Nonetheless, Achilles' pity for Patroclus' grief over the Achaeans' predicament indicates that Achilles still has, by extension, some feeling of obligation to his former fellow warriors. Gregory Nagy characterizes the Homeric relationship of comradeship in these terms of obligation: "This warrior society," Nagy writes, "… sets the ethical standards of our *Iliad* in terms of the bonds that unite the …members." Homer's term for these members is *philioi*, which translates as "friends."[18]

Achilles' experience forms a pattern clearly recognizable in studies of the wars of modern times. The stages of Achilles' experience form a recurring cyclical pattern frequently reported by 20th century war veterans. In his book *Achilles in Vietnam*, the sociologist Jonathan Shay has documented the ways in which the stages of Achilles' experience overlap with stages of experience reported by Vietnam combat veterans suffering post-traumatic stress. A commander's betrayal of what is right, social withdrawal, the death of a close comrade, berserk rampage and the desire to mutilate the enemy's corpse form a recurrent sequence in these narratives.[19]

---

18 Nagy, *The Best of the Achaeans*, 83.
19 Shay, Jonathan. 1994. *Achilles in Vietnam: Combat Trauma and the Undoing of Character*. New York: Scribner Books. See also Shay, Jonathan. 1991. "Learn-

Achilles cannot admit to Patroclus his longing to aid his former comrades, because Achilles has a **far stronger emotion: rage**. Achilles has suffered his commander Agamemnon's betrayal of what is right.[20] Jonathan Shay offers a number of comparable examples in the narratives of Vietnam veterans, many of whom upon their return experienced rage at being blamed by their fellow Americans for their role in perpetuating an unpopular war, despite their individual sacrifices and accomplishments. Shay compares this to the rage at being betrayed by a commander in the field:

> The rage is the same, whether it is fairness, so valued by Americans, or honor, the highest good of Homer's officers, that has been violated.... In both cases the moral constitution of the army, its cultural contract, has been impaired.[21]

In Shay's study, soldiers who experience rage in the form of this indignant wrath find it very difficult to recover, because this rage destroys social bonds and forces the betrayed warrior into isolation. The Greek word for this particular rage, *menis*, associates it with something divine precisely because it separates the warrior who experiences it from the human community. Shay concludes that "Homer uses *menis* only as the word for the rage that ruptures social attachments."[22] Achilles' withdrawal from the Greek army is

---

ing about Combat Stress from Homer's *Iliad*," *Journal of Traumatic Stress*, 4.4: 561-579.

20 Here, 'what is right' can refer both to what is due Achilles' merit and to what satisfies the moral requirements of justice. This latter sense is anachronistic to the *Iliad* but useful for today's reader. See Adkins, A. W. H. 1960. *Merit and Responsibility: A Study in Greek Values*. Oxford: Clarendon Press, for an account of how moral responsibility develops out of the notion of heroic merit in the centuries after Homer's epics were composed.

21 Shay, *Achilles in Vietnam*, 14.

22 Ibid, 21.

a direct consequence of his rage. Yet, while Achilles feels betrayed by Agamemnon, the other heroes perceive his withdrawal itself as a betrayal: Achilles has abandoned the comrades he once served as champion and defender. Achilles attempts to cope with the conflict between his outrage and his ethical feelings of obligation to his fellow warriors by employing an all-too human response: denial.

Achilles' state of denial is apparent to the reader during the diplomatic meeting in Achilles' tent in Book Nine. In this meeting, Achilles rejects outright the offers of recompense presented by Odysseus and Phoenix. The third speaker, Ajax, makes no such offers, but instead expresses the heartbreak and the betrayal he has felt at Achilles' withdrawal from the fighting. At the beginning, Ajax does not even address Achilles, but declares his bitterness to his fellow ambassadors:

> "There's no achieving our mission here, I see,
> not with this approach. Best to return at once,
> give the Achaeans a full report, defeating as it is…
> Achilles – he's made his own proud spirit so wild in his chest,
> So savage, not a thought for his comrade's love –
> Here we are,
> Under your roof, sent from the whole Achaean force!
> Past all other men, all other Achaean comrades,
> We long to be your closest, dearest friends" (9. 763-785)

In contrast to the exhortations of Odysseus and Phoenix, Ajax' bitter words have an immediate effect on Achilles, who responds by modifying his earlier declaration that he will sail home. Stung by what Ajax has said, Achilles hurriedly announces a new decision - he will stay in Troy but only fight when the danger threatens his own ships.

Achilles' decision to remain at Troy but fight only out of self-interest does not resolve anything; it leaves Achilles in stasis with respect not just to his identity as a warrior but with respect to the prophecy of Zeus. This prophecy requires Achilles to choose either an anonymous homecoming and civilian life, or the honor of death in battle. Although Thetis and Achilles repeatedly invoke this prophecy (1.496 – 498, 603; 9. 499-505), neither of them takes seriously the possibility that Achilles might choose to return home. Achilles made his choice when he sailed to Troy. In response to Odysseus' speech during the embassy, once it is clear that Agamemnon does not intend to apologize, Achilles tests out the possibility of making a different choice: he declares that he will sail away from Troy and return to a life of peace, without honor. When Ajax rejects him for this final betrayal, Achilles quickly changes his mind. Achilles' new decision, however, is not a choice offered by the prophecy. The decision to remain at Troy but fight only out of self-interest leaves Achilles without hope of resolution, exposed to all the censure of his former comrades, but without any hope of restoring his peacetime intimacies.[23]

Achilles' inability to choose a long, peaceful life away from the arena in which honor is earned reflects the persistent and powerful

---

23 Odysseus notices this as well and does not interpret Achilles' new intention as a concession. He reports to Agamemnon only that Achilles has decided to go home. Achilles' departure would put him out of reach of Agamemnon's authority but Achilles' staying at Troy on these new terms merely reaffirms his rejection of Agamemnon's command. Just as Odysseus diplomatically refrained from repeating to Achilles Agamemnon's call for submission, so he refrains from telling Agamemnon the full extent of Achilles' insubordination.

ambivalence that many born warriors feel for peacetime. Peace is not exciting. Peacetime cannot provide extreme stimulation at the ongoing levels that are routine in combat. Paradoxically, there is a part of human nature that fears peace for its stasis and for the listlessness of the social virtues displayed by a community at peace. J. Glenn Gray accounts for this paradox as follows:

> We are often puzzled by our combined failure to enlist in the pursuit of a peaceful world the unified effort, cheerfulness in sacrifice, determination, and persistence that arise almost spontaneously in the pursuit of war…. The majority of us, restless and unfulfilled, see no supreme worth in our present state. We want more out of life than we are getting and are always half-ready to chance everything on the realization of great expectations.[24]

The moral guidelines of Christianity and the law of armed conflict teach us to be suspicious of those who admit to enjoying the lures of combat. In Ernest Hemingway's short story "Soldier's Home," Krebs, who enjoyed his time in combat in World War I, finds that he is expected to lie about this back home in the American Midwest, the so-called "Bible belt."[25] Only recently have we formed a view of war addiction as a psychological condition, and developed therapy for those who want to forfeit their futures for the intoxication of combat. Consider, for example, the 2008 film "The Hurt Locker," which called the public's attention to this form of PTSD in soldiers who had fought in Iraq. Chris Hedges' famous

---

24 Gray, *The Warriors*, 215.
25 Hemingway, Ernest. 1925. "Soldier's Home." https://www.somanybooks.org/eng208/SoldiersHome.pdf

quote "war is a drug" flashes across the screen as an epigram at the beginning of the film, and in the final scene, the protagonist chooses an almost certain, premature death on the bomb squad over a quiet, peacetime life with his loving and bewildered family.

The decision to stay at Troy but fight only out of self-interest, the decision that Achilles hastily composes at the end of Book 9, leaves him in stasis; it resolves nothing. This stasis stalls Homer's plot as well, which spins its wheels for seven books until Achilles agrees to send Patroclus into battle in his place. In order to understand why Achilles takes this particular action to break the stasis, let us return to the conversation between Patroclus and Achilles at the beginning of Book Sixteen.

Patroclus responds to Achilles' mocking simile of the baby girl with a taunt of his own. Patroclus now exploits Achilles' dilemma by implying that Achilles is afraid to fight. Has the prophecy made his friend a coward, afraid to face death in combat?

> But still, if down deep some prophecy makes you balk
> Some doom your noble mother revealed to you from Zeus,
> Well and good: at least send me into battle, quickly (16. 37-43)

For Patroclus, the suffering of his former comrades is now a sufficient reason to fight. Patroclus, who has hitherto stayed out of fighting in order to support his comrade's grievance against Agamemnon, is now eager to overlook Agamemnon's insult and return to battle because of his compassion for the wounded Achaean warriors.

Achilles responds immediately and defensively to Patroclus' taunt:

No, no, my prince, Patroclus, what are you saying? Prophecies?
None that touch me. None I know of. No doom my noble
mother revealed to me from Zeus, just this terrible pain that
wounds me to the quick – when one man attempts to plunder
a man his equal, to commandeer a prize, exulting so in his own
power. That's the pain that wounds me, suffering such humil-
iation. That girl – the sons of Achaea picked her as my prize,
and I'd sacked a walled city, won her with my spear but right
from my grasp he tears her, mighty Agamemnon, that son of
Atreus! Treating me like some vagabond, some outcast stripped
of all my rights… Enough. Let bygones be bygones now. Done
is done. How on earth can a man rage on forever? Still, by god,
I said I would not relax my anger, not till the cries and carnage
reached my own ships (16. 57-72).

According to Achilles in this speech, it is not the prophecy but his
concern for his own word that keeps Achilles out of battle. Achilles is consumed by his grievance with Agamemnon to the extent
that he distorts his own words in Book Nine into a binding vow
that holds him back from the fighting. Achilles attempts to draw
attention away from his ethically compromising decision only to
fight out of self-interest by citing the need to stand by his word.
Unlike Agamemnon, who gives and then takes back, Achilles will
be a man of his word.

Achilles now clearly has the urge to return to battle. He makes
a distinction he was unwilling to make when he sent Patroclus
to find out who had been wounded. While Achilles then held all
the Achaeans guilty by association, here he distinguishes between
the warrior community who bestowed Briseis and the individual

Agamemnon who took her away. Although his resentment toward Agamemnon persists, Achilles now reinstates the rest of the Achaeans as his worthy comrades. Trapped by a dilemma that he had a role in creating, Achilles agrees to send Patroclus to battle in his place and in his armor.

The hybrid figure of Patroclus in Achilles' armor is traditionally interpreted as a representation of the divided man that Achilles has become. Because of the unresolved circumstances surrounding Agamemnon's insult, Achilles can only send a façade of himself into this battle – if we interpret his armor as a symbol of the pitiless façade Achilles once put on only for the Trojans but which he now extends to his own comrades as well. Under this façade, the compassionate Patroclus represents Achilles' hidden desire to aid and assist those former comrades.

Once Patroclus is ceremoniously clad in Achilles' armor, Achilles gives him a command that will be impossible for Patroclus to obey: "You must not, lost in the flush and fire of triumph, slaughtering Trojans outright, drive your troops to Troy…. No, you must turn back – soon as you bring the light of victory to the ships" (16. 107-114). Achilles gives two apparently contradictory reasons for this order. The first is that Achilles' honor would be diminished if his stand-in Patroclus had too much success in battle. The second reason is that Achilles still dreams, despite the prophecy, that he and Patroclus might storm Troy side by side: "Oh would to god… we could bring Troy's hallowed crown of towers toppling down around us – you and I alone!" (16. 115-119). This personal fantasy, an apotheosis of the comrade relationship, is incompatible with the actual prophecy, which decrees that Achilles will die before Troy is taken. However, Achilles' wishful thinking here reveals how painful it will be for him to stay behind, still inactive.

Whatever Achilles' motives, this command is antithetical to Patroclus' own heroic nature. Given the depth of their intimacy, why does Achilles not understand that Patroclus will not and cannot leave the battle voluntarily without compromising his own honor? Achilles acknowledges this only belatedly in his soliloquy of foreboding at the beginning of Book Eighteen.

Achilles has remained ignorant of the death of Patroclus throughout Book Seventeen. Because he can see that the fighting is far off, under the walls of Troy, Achilles does not suspect the death of his friend until he sees the Greeks in retreat at the end of Book Seventeen. Antilochus brings him the news of Patroclus' death at the beginning of Book Eighteen, at which time Achilles is already experiencing "foreboding." Even as Antilochus races up to him, Achilles delivers a soliloquy addressed "to his own great heart":

Why, why? Our long-haired Achaeans routed again,
driven in terror off the plain to crowd the ships, but why?
Dear Gods, don't bring to pass the grief that haunts my heart –
The prophecy that mother revealed to me one time…
She said the best of the Myrmidons – while I lived –
Would fall at Trojan hands and leave the light of day.
And now he's dead, I know it. Menoetius' gallant son,
My headstrong friend!…(18. 6-13).

Achilles' disclosure of this new prophecy, at this point in events, is shocking. Why have we not heard of it before now? Even if Achilles did not think about it consciously, the Freudian conclusion seems warranted – surely Achilles was subconsciously aware that he was sending Patroclus to his death? Perhaps as a result of his selective memory, this prophecy "haunts" Achilles' heart and he now acknowledges that Patroclus' death in this battle would be its obvious fulfillment.

There is also something disturbingly Freudian about the manner in which this prophecy comes to be fulfilled. Although it can be reformulated to mean that the second-best of the Myrmidons – Patroclus - will die during Achilles' lifetime, the literal meaning is that the man who will die will be the best of the Myrmidons – that is, Achilles - and yet Achilles will remain paradoxically alive. Menelaos, in reporting Patroclus' death to Antilochus, is attentive to this problem of how to attribute full heroic honors to Patroclus while Achilles is still alive. "The best of the Achaeans has been killed," Menelaos begins, and then stops to qualify, "Patroklos, that is…" (17.689-90).[26] As we have seen, Patroclus represents the most social elements of Achilles' character: his compassion for his fellow warriors and his still-active desire to serve as their champion. With Patroclus' death, this part of Achilles dies as well and he transforms into a berserk killer.

Achilles' berserk rage is distinct from the indignant wrath he felt earlier, although this berserk rage too tears apart the social fabric of communal experience. Berserk rage converts grief, guilt and hurt into blind hate. The quote I mentioned earlier from a Vietnam veteran calls attention to the irresistibility of this emotional sequence: "Even now, I cannot fully explain this barbarous equation: I felt pain, rage, and then I wanted to kill someone."[27]

---

26 Nagy, *The Best of the Achaeans*, 63.
27 Anderson, *When War Becomes Personal*, 144.

As we have seen, Achilles' grief is intensified by the circumstances of his own stasis, which leads to his approving Patroclus' request to go to battle in his stead, thereby providing a ready-made role for Patroclus' well-documented spirit of self-sacrifice. In J. Glenn Gray's analysis of comradeship, the willingness to sacrifice oneself is made during the intensity of battle and is thus accompanied by the suppressed sense of self that distinguishes comradeship from friendship. This analysis applies to the extent that Patroclus longs to fight in the aid of his former Achaean comrades. Patroclus' role in helping Achilles find resolution for his intolerable stasis appears in a different light. Given Patroclus' established capacity for empathy and intimacy, we might expect him to think that only his death in this stage of the combat will give Achilles the incentive to return to the terms of the hero cult and seek the prophesied death that will bring him honor. Patroclus' death will serve two goals: it will secure his own heroic status, while providing Achilles with an undeniable reason to shake off his indignation with Agamemnon and return to combat, namely, the spirit of revenge. Three features of Homer's narrative support this suggestion that Patroclus may enter this battle seeking an opportunity for an intentional self-sacrifice. One of these is Homer's depiction of Patroclus as uniquely responsive to the needs of Achilles; another the figurative way in which Homer foreshadows Patroclus' death; and finally Homer's unique direct addresses to Patroclus that include the powerful epithetic address "O my rider" (see 16. 682, 810, 867, 915).

In Book Eleven, Homer portrays Patroclus as unquestioningly attentive to Achilles' needs:

He called at once to his friend-in-arms Patroclus, shouting down
from the decks. Hearing Achilles, forth he came from his shelter,
striding up like the deathless god of war but from that moment
on his doom was sealed. The brave son of Menoetius spoke out
first: "why do you call, Achilles? Do you need me?" (11. 710-16)

Here Homer links Patroclus' death to his responsiveness to Achilles.
Patroclus is known for his compassion; he is attuned to the needs
of others, but particularly to the needs of Achilles. In this passage,
Achilles ostensibly needs Patroclus only to go as a messenger to
learn which of the Greek warriors has been wounded. Achilles' real
need, however, is to find a way out of the stasis that holds him and
Patroclus from their honor. Here, Homer's language conveys both
of these levels of meaning, as well as the way this summons initi-
ates an irrevocable chain of events that will lead to Patroclus' death.

Homer himself gives preferential treatment to Patroclus, the
only human character addressed by the bardic narrator in the second
person. Homer's only other use of direct address is to the divine
muse in the opening line of the epic. Homer's special feeling for
Patroclus seems linked to Patroclus' self-sacrifice, for this direct
address appears only in Book Sixteen as Patroclus approaches his
death.

For whatever reasons, Homer's narrative devices establish Patroclus as a character worthy of the extraordinary mourning that
bestows divinity on the highest heroes according to the terms of
the hero cult. Achilles' response to the loss of Patroclus could not
be more extreme. This unendurable grief foreshadows the grief to
be suffered by the survivors upon the prophesied death of Achil-

les, and illustrates the inhumane demand of the Homeric hero cult that honor be purchased by grief that must be ever intensifying.

Because of the prophecy, Achilles' decision to come to Troy was a choice to die in combat. Because of Agamemnon's insult and Achilles' subsequent withdrawal, Achilles had to make this choice a second time under much more painful circumstances. Renunciation of heroic honor was not possible for Achilles, but to attain it required the sacrifice of Patroclus. Achilles' subsequent berserk and bestial rampage is his response to a profound existential dilemma that requires him to choose between two unacceptable options: renounce immortal honor or suffer the loss of his beloved comrade and friend. In order to keep his honor, Achilles must choose unbearable grief. His rage at the terms of this choice propel him to his savage killing spree and his bestial act of mutilating Hector's corpse.

Such savagery and bestiality continues to be well-documented in combat. Progress in moral theory and notions of military justice have not helped warriors navigate the extreme responses that the bonds of comradeship can trigger. Media coverage of the wars in Iraq and Afghanistan has documented many cases of killing sprees, prisoner abuse, and mutilation of an enemy's corpse done in the spirit of retaliation. Clearly, the terms of Achilles' choice still resonate in the modern war environment. The persistence of the pattern of Achilles' experience in narratives from Vietnam, Iraq, Afghanistan and other recent wars can help us understand the traumatic potential inherent in subjecting the warrior to an intense and prolonged conflict between honor and intimacy. By the Law of Armed Conflict, a soldier's honor requires controlling his impulse to avenge his comrades, bottling up any grief, shame, guilt, or rage he might feel at his own inability to protect them. We now know that asking a soldier to confine these intense emotions, without the prospect of therapeutic release, to some inner compartment, some untouchable inner space that is the original meaning of Brian Turner's phrase "the Hurt Locker," can psychologically shatter a young soldier as effectively as a court martial for war crimes could destroy his reputation.[28]

The warzone relationship of comradeship is not comparable to any peacetime relationship. J. Glenn Gray distinguishes it from friendship, for it does not have time to build on the uniqueness of the individuals involved, but has to proceed under the constant threat of death. The interrelationship between honor and grief persists in the terms established by Homer's *Iliad*, and this irony, this constant and imminent danger of loss of one's intimates continues to give structure to the bonds between soldiers. For the Western soldier, the shared ideals of honor and country are subsumed in combat by a feeling for their comrades-in-arms that is made more intense by the prospect of loss. For the individual soldiers, honor in combat is earned through acting out one's connections to one's fellows, while knowing that this intimacy has a high probability of coming to grief.

The agonizing terms of Achilles' choice still resonate in the western military environment that now defines honor as an internal moral quality rather than as the ritual reward given posthumously to a fallen hero. Wherever the individual warrior can be honored by his comrades' displays of intimacy, the war zone will evoke some facsimile of the experiential relationship between honor

---

28 Turner, Brian. 2005. "The Hurt Locker." https://www.poetryfoundation.org/poems/54141/the-hurt-locker

and grief that characterized Homeric warfare. If we remove the divine mandates of the Homeric hero cult and the Homeric gods, Homer's *Iliad* can help us understand the conflicting demands that honor and intimacy continue to make on a warrior.[29] The Homeric relationship between honor and grief offers us an interpretive model with which to approach the more fluid and perhaps more poignant contemporary connection between the ethical and moral demands of honor and the personal experience of loss. The character of Achilles should teach us a healthy respect for the intense power of the grief, pain, and rage that can be released in combat, in worlds, as Hector's mother knows and fears, that are far from hot baths, wine, and the comfort of loved ones.

---

29 Lefkowitz, Mary. 2003. *Greek Gods, Human Lives: What We can Learn from Myths*. New Haven: Yale University Press.

Chapter 3

Herodotus: A Multicultural Approach

The English philosopher David Hume wrote in 1739 that during wartime it is human nature to vilify our enemies and esteem our own virtues:

> When our own nation is at war with any other, we detest them under the character of cruel, perfidious, unjust and violent: But always esteem ourselves and allies equitable, moderate, and merciful.[1]

The ideological portrayal of a stark conflict between the cultures of democracy and tyranny is well documented both in contemporary Western war narratives and Cold War rhetoric. Tom Clancy's 1984 best seller, *The Hunt for Red October*, illustrates the rhetorical association of the West with innovation and flexibility of mind, and Soviet Russia with slavish and violent intent. The end of the Cold War and the multi-polar global dynamic that has ensued has brought a renewed interest in cultivating a more dynamic mode of cross-cultural discourse, with a resurgence of interest in Herodotus, the early Greek historian, who tells in his *History* the story of how Greece was invaded in the early 5th century BCE by two

---

1   Hume, David. 1978. *A Treatise of Human Nature*. Edited by P. H. Nidditch. Oxford: Oxford University Press, 348.

successive armies under autocratic Persian rule.[2] While popular media portrayals, like the 2006 film *300*, depict these invasions as classic showdowns between freedom and tyranny, a close look at Herodotus' *History* shows a more nuanced reality. The two sides have many features in common, with individuals on both sides acquiring and wielding power in similar ways. Herodotus demonstrates an attentiveness to cultural differences that enables him to implement an open-minded, multi-polar inquiry that has been criticized by ancients and moderns alike for its lack of intellectual rigor. These critiques overlook Herodotus' own goal of conveying diverse cultural traditions in their own terms. Herodotus does not impose on his narrative the authority of an overriding analytic reason and the prerequisite of a unified, coherent perspective that accompanies it.

Herodotus approaches the genre of history with the working assumption that no single paradigm or perspective will suffice to capture the clash of cultures that the Persian Wars represent, where those involved used different idioms to classify and make sense of their experience. In this situation, the historian must make a choice about which perspective to offer the reader, knowing that readers will take it forward as a model with which to make sense of the next conflict. Herodotus deliberately avoids a unitary perspective. He is transparent about his own choices of what to include, and he enables us to see for ourselves how he utilizes his powers of discrimination. In his writing, questions about the acquisition and wielding

---

2   In 2007, Robert Strassler published his new translation. (Strassler, Robert. 2009. *The Landmark Herodotus*. New York: Anchor Books), and Robert Kaplan argued for Herodotus' importance in "A Historian for Our Time" (*The Atlantic* Jan/Feb 2007. Web).

of power emerge primarily as language problems, problems thus inescapably tied in to the historian's own methods in structuring and presenting the narrative. Herodotus sets out a liberal model for developing a strategic sense based on the ability to assess one's opponents on multiple levels simultaneously, and on the ability to be self-conscious about the narrative one constructs on the basis of these assessments. His work offers us a multidimensional model that remains crucial today, when Herodotus' dictum "culture is king" sums up the diversity that characterizes social and political life.

Herodotus' opening passage contains some clues about his multicultural and multidisciplinary methodology:

> I, Herodotus of Halicarnassus, am here showing forth my history, that time may not draw the color from what man has brought into being, nor those great and wonderful deeds, manifested by both Greeks and barbarians, fail of their report... (*Hist.* 1.1).[3]

In his opening lines, Herodotus introduces us to the Greek word *historia*, from which our English word 'history' derives. Since Herodotus is among the first to use this word, we deduce much of its meaning from him. Based on Herodotus' usage, Liddell and Scott's Greek lexicon translates *historia* as "a learning by inquiry, a narration of what one has learnt."[4] This definition says nothing about 'the facts', or the accuracy of the historical narrative. Nonetheless, Herodotus' claim to show forth a history raises expectations

---

3   All translations are from Herodotus. 1987. *The History*. Translated by David Grene. Chicago: University of Chicago Press.
4   Liddell, Henry George and Robert Scott. 2019. *Greek-English Lexicon*. Oxford: Clarendon Press.

about the accuracy and objectivity of his account, for Herodotus understood history as a descriptive genre; the "great and wonderful deeds" he claims to "show forth" in the quote above remained in living memory at the time of his writing. After reading only a few pages of Herodotus' history, a critical modern reader will have to examine her expectations, because the author is not a rigorous historian in the modern sense, and he does not assure his reader that he has verified his sources or his facts. For a modern reader, the question invariably arises: is Herodotus a legitimate historian?

Herodotus views the rise of the Persian and Greek powers as the result of two complex ethnic systems, each composed of dynamic, often irrational elements that interacted in unexpected ways. The Greek city-states accounted for their histories to a large extent in mythical terms. Among the Persians, the story of Cyrus' consolidation of the Persian Empire was similarly shrouded in myth and legend. Herodotus' historical narrative thus strikes modern readers as something closer to a story then a history, for it is filled with the sort of myths, legendary remnants of the oral tradition, and digressions that fall more into the domain of anthropology than that of modern historiography.

Herodotus tellingly expresses concern not that time will falsify the memory of the events of the Persian Wars, but that time will "draw the color" from their report. Unlike Thucydides, who only 50 years later criticized Herodotus for not using his reason to distinguish more rigorously fact from fiction, Herodotus does not attempt to establish a rational advantage over his sources. Limited as he is by the oral nature of his research, his inquiry is not so much into what happened as into what people say about what happened.

Listening to what people say is an activity Herodotus takes seriously for its own sake, he believes that the ongoing representation of the deed in speech is as important as the one-time deed. This approach enabled Herodotus to give an account of the complex web of social, legal, economic, political and religious factors that comprised each culture's understanding of its own identity.

In the opening passage quoted above, Herodotus describes his act of writing as a "showing forth." He shows forth an account of the Persian Wars derived from stories told to him orally. Herodotus lets us know that his research entailed extensive travels, and consisted mainly in collecting oral retellings of these events from both eyewitnesses and second-hand reporters. In his research activity, Herodotus shows great respect for oral transmission, and does not make much of a distinction between 'accounts' and 'stories'. Indeed, he transmits many stories we might call trivial, even mythical, and often passes on contradictory stories about the same event. His focus in doing this is not on finding out what stories are accurate, but on finding out what stories are still told (e.g. 7. 152). If a story is still told, Herodotus grants it a kind of truth for having become part of the tradition. To many modern readers, this method may appear to lack objectivity. We would like Herodotus to be more discriminating and to reject stories that are too obviously colored by myth, tradition, and bias. We need to look closely at why Herodotus did not choose to develop his powers of discrimination this way

As the 20th century philosopher Martin Heidegger pointed out, the literal meaning of the Greek word for truth, *aletheia*, is "not concealed."[5] The original sense of 'truth' was not objective truth,

---

5 Heidegger, Martin. 2019. *Being and Time*. Translated by John Macquarrie and Edward Robinson. New York: Harper & Row, 56-7.

but the perspectival truth we grant to all sincere narratives. Heidegger describes this original meaning as "letting something be seen."[6] This perspectival truth is not the same as fiction; it is closer to the multicultural perspective we cultivate today. Paul Hirst makes this point in his objection to Samuel Huntington's thesis of a 'clash of civilizations':

> There is little prospect of the 'clash of civilizations' propounded by Samuel Huntington. The main reason is that civilizations are not homogeneous enough to group the world according to such values… This does not mean that the West must subscribe to extreme cultural relativism… It does mean that we must recognize that there are other legitimate idioms in which respect for toleration, liberty and justice can be expressed.[7]

Hirst here distinguishes between an extreme cultural relativism, in which we must respect all individuals' beliefs equally, and a considered **multiculturalism**, in which we accept that other cultures may have different modes for interpreting the universal values of freedom and order. As we go on, we shall see that Herodotus made this distinction as well. He reserves his judgment of both Persian autocracy and Greek democracy until he has researched and reported the both peoples' own narratives.

Although Herodotus does not edit his material with the goal of obtaining a singular and objective truth, there is something objective in his method. The objectivity in Herodotus' activity lies not in the

---

6   Ibid.
7   Hirst, Paul. 2015. *War and Power in the 21ˢᵗ Century*. Cambridge: Polity Press, 100.

content, but in the conduct of the inquiry.[8] Herodotus' integrity is his very lack of discrimination, his willingness to listen to any story and write it down. Adopting the motto "custom is king," Herodotus collects his material with open interest and personal curiosity. In this activity, he carries out his investigations *freely*.

Greece is known for a rich and long-lived oral tradition, in which cultural lore was transmitted formulaically through epic story-cycles like Homer's *Iliad* and *Odyssey*. The move from orality to literacy enabled the Greeks to set about interpreting their world in multidimensional ways.[9] Eric Havelock has shown that it was Plato, at the beginning of the 4th century BCE, who capitalized on the "keen analysis or dissection of the world and of thought itself made possible by the interiorizing of the alphabet in the Greek psyche."[10] Plato's preference for a single, overriding, analytic account determined by the rational authority of the author was the exception, not the norm.

Although he derived much of his evidence orally, Herodotus in his *History* does more than transmit the oral tradition. After collecting oral accounts, Herodotus does have to choose how to present them. He generates his written account as a carefully constructed narrative, stamped with his own interpretation, by means of which the Persian Wars will appear "in living color" to all who can read the Greek language. In departing from the strict, rigid formulae of the Homeric oral tradition, Herodotus begins an inquiry into

---

8   "The universal logos which Herodotus tries to uncover lies completely embedded in the particulars that he narrates… [The argument] shows both what it is and how Herodotus arrived at it." Benardete, Seth. 2009. *Herodotean Inquiries*. South Bend: St. Augustine's Press, 4.

9   Ong, Walter J. 1988. *Orality and Literacy: The Technologizing of the Word*. London: Methuen Books.

10 Quoted by Ong, *Orality and Literacy*, 28.

the generative potential of language, and he readily acknowledges that his own account is just one of many possible ways to give new life to the past (1. 95). Herodotus does not entertain notions of his own absolute objectivity and rational authority. This gives the reader a unique ability to make, as well as to withhold, judgment. In surrendering her expectation of objectivity, the reader gains in return a methodological transparency that grants her the ability to question and evaluate the evidence for herself. Herodotus intends his reader not to rush to replace this transparency with an interpretive judgment of her own, but to encounter the diversity of perspectives with a sense of wonder. Like Montaigne would do in the 16th century with his interest in the exploratory essay as a genre, Herodotus urges us to take the time to marvel at human diversity, and to call elements of our own paradigm into question through our encounter with radically different customs.[11]

Thus Herodotus (unlike his successor Thucydides) does not wield his newfound power from behind the scenes, but allows us to see for ourselves how language functions in his text, particularly in the first book of the *History*. In Book One, Herodotus displays for us the evolution of his account, and offers a kind of documentary of how his own understanding of language as history evolved. In his tales of Croesus, Cyrus, the Spartans, Athenians and Ionians, Herodotus develops the theme that language has a power that goes beyond truth-telling, a generative power that bestows identity and authority on a man or a people. Throughout Book One, the power of men and nations (Greek and the perceived "barbarian" alike) manifests itself as an attitude toward language.

11 Montaigne, Michel. 1958. *The Complete Essays of Montaigne*. Translated by Donald M. Frame. Stanford: Stanford University Press.

Herodotus' sensitivity to the generative power of language allows him to resist much of the rhetorical oversimplification of the Persians as mere barbarians. Some such oversimplification may be inevitable. "People are always tempted," comments Samuel Huntington, "to divide people into us and them, the in-group and the other, our civilization and those barbarians."[12] In Herodotus' day, the Persians were viewed as belonging to the barbarian peoples. Palestinian literary critic Edward Said's critique of contemporary political anti-Muslim campaigns applies as well to the tendency, strong in Herodotus' own day, to identify the Greeks with civilization and the Persians with barbarism:

> As rallying cries for their constituencies, "Islam" and "the West" (or "America") provide incitement more than insight. As equal and opposite reactions to the disorientations of new actualities, "Islam" and "the West" can turn analysis into simple polemic, experience into fantasy. Respect for the concrete detail of human experience, understanding that arises from viewing the Other compassionately, knowledge gained and diffused through moral and intellectual honesty: surely these are better, if not easier, goals at present than confrontation and reductive hostility. And if in the process we can dispose finally of both the residual hatred and the offensive generality of labels like "the Muslim," "the Persian," "the Turk," "the Arab," or "the Westerner," then so much the better.[13]

---

12 Huntington, Samuel. 2011. *The Clash of Civilizations*. New York: Simon & Schuster, 32.
13 Said, Edward. 1981. *Covering Islam: How the Media and the Experts Determine How We See the Rest of the World*. New York: Pantheon Books, xxxi.

This residual hatred against the Persians, and the popular use of rhetorical labels of enmity applied to the barbarian culture, was endemic in antiquity, and Herodotus came under considerable attack for his attempt to look past the generalized prejudice. In the 1st century CE the Greek essayist and biographer Plutarch published an essay entitled "On the Malice of Herodotus," accusing Herodotus of being *philobarbarus*, a lover of the barbarians.[14] Ancient discourse was, like today's, driven by a set of mono-cultural prejudices hostile to conscious and deliberate multicultural practices.

Herodotus' first case study in Book One of the *History* is the story of Croesus, the leader of Lydia whom Cyrus conquered in his consolidation of the Persian Empire. In the terms of Herodotus' narrative, Croesus was the victim of fate. Herodotus tells us that Croesus was fated to fall, although the details of Herodotus' story link this fate to the way Croesus was handicapped by his limited understanding of language. Croesus takes a rigidly linear approach to problems and puzzles of strategy, and he fails to acknowledge that terms can have non-literal meanings. His story can be read as a fable cautioning against a strategic disregard for the unpredictable or unexpected, a fable whose moral is that those ruled by the necessity of their own idealized paradigms will fail.

Croesus' story illustrates that the art of interpretation requires a certain level of diversity in order to develop. As Rousseau points out, "Reflection is born of the comparison of ideas, and it is the plurality of ideas that leads to their comparison."[15] By this account,

---

14 Plutarch. 1965. *Moralia, Volume XI: On the Malice of Herodotus. Causes of Natural Phenomena*. Translated by Lionel Pearson and F. H. Sandbach. Cambridge, MA: Harvard University Press, 2-132.

15 Rousseau, Jean-Jacques. 1966. "Essay on the Origin of Languages." In *On the Origin of Language*. Translated by John Moran and Alexander Gode. Chicago: University of Chicago Press, 32.

Croesus' lack of exposure to diversity would have worked against him, for "those whose experience remains confined to the narrow range of their childhood also are incapable of such comparisons."[16]

Herodotus describes how the fall of Lydia and the rise of Persia was a geopolitical event that entailed a move away from mythic notions of fated behavior, and toward a tradition of rational inquiry and rational explanation. In order to become a historical people, in order to claim their heritage and destiny as their own, the early Persians had first to free themselves from a world view in which supernatural, unpredictable forces had influence over human affairs. The story of the rise of the Persian Empire is a story about individuals coming to understand themselves as human beings who could find their own appropriate responses to uncertainty, utilize their opportunities, and find creative solutions even to the problem of their own identity. As Rousseau would observe in the 18th century, such a self-conception is accompanied by a concomitant growth in the capacity to use language creatively and with an awareness of its many layers. An appropriately modulated response requires a language capable of an equivalent range of meaning, a language that is fluid and can adapt itself to complex circumstances.

Lacking such a language, Croesus is somehow trapped in between the mythic and the rational. While apparently bound by divine necessity, he is simultaneously not a creature of myth because his actions and their consequences are subject to the rational laws of cause-and-effect. For this reason, Herodotus grants Croesus the status of emerging as the first historical figure in the narrative of the origins of the conflict between Persia and Greece. Croesus is the first individual whom Herodotus will "set [his] mark upon:"

---

16 Ibid.

> For my part, I am not going to say about these matters that they
> happened thus or thus, but I will set my mark upon that man
> that I myself know began unjust acts against the Greeks, and,
> having so marked him, I will go forward in my account... (1. 5)

Despite Croesus' fated failure, his war against the Greeks had both known cause and known effect. This ambiguity enables us to read into Croesus' story a metaphor of a man bound to necessities of his own making, a man who lacks insight to such a breathtaking extent that we associate his blindness with hubris. Upon his query of the oracles at Delphi and Amphiaraos whether he should invade Persia, Croesus received the response that if he did so he would destroy a great empire (1.53). Unable to perceive the obvious ambiguity in this reply, Croesus' single-minded pursuit of an invasion of Persia takes its place alongside other ill-fated expeditions of conquest that have come to represent blind hubris. Many recent accounts of military expeditions in Iraq and Vietnam similarly make their failures look, in retrospect, as inevitable as Croesus' loss of Lydia.[17]

If we connect this to Herodotus' opening passage, it continues to clarify what Herodotus means by *historia*. Croesus is the first historical figure whose actions can be studied for what they brought about. The Herodotean project of history takes shape around the conflict between divine necessity and human autonomy, or between human blindness and human insight, both conflicts that Croesus' story epitomizes. Historical narrative requires a sense of oneself in time, a sense that demands that explanations based on rational cause

---

17 See, e.g., McMasters, H. R.. 1997. *Dereliction of Duty*. New York: HarperCollins; Cloud and Jaffe, *The Fourth Star*; and Ricks, Thomas. 2006. *Fiasco: The American Military Adventure in Iraq*. London: Penguin Press.

and effect be available, that events have a sequence that reason can comprehend. In Herodotus' narrative, individuals in the West and East alike struggle to navigate a balance between divine necessity and individual autonomy. Croesus, Herodotus' first example of such an individual, remains oblivious to ambiguities that are obvious to Herodotus' readers.

For example, having dreamt that his son Atys will die by an iron spear, Croesus forbids his son to go on the boar hunt where the boy longs to "find renown" as a hero. Atys protests with an argument based on the most literal reading of the dream: a boar has no spear. Concluding his argument, Atys gives his father a choice: "Either let me go to the hunt, or let your words convince me that this action of yours is for the best" (1. 37). Croesus responds, "My son, somehow you overcome my judgment in your reading of the dream" (1. 40). With this 'somehow', Croesus betrays his unease. Although he senses that Atys' argument that a boar has no spear is mere quibbling, Croesus is unable or unwilling to construct an argument that would prevent Atys from acting.

Croesus' silence here, his inability to formulate his foreboding into a persuasive argument, is an indicator of his lack of freedom. Croesus is unwilling to depart from his linear thought-process in order to construct an argument based on something unexpected. In this situation, interpretation is impossible for him, and he sees only two choices: to surrender his judgment altogether to the prophecy or to defy it in the most literal-minded way. Croesus chooses the latter, allows himself to be persuaded by Atys' literal reading of the prophecy, and loses his son to the unexpected contingency of an errant spear thrown by a fellow huntsman.

In another example, Croesus approaches his own fate with similar blindness. When he considers the possibility of invading Persia to expand his empire, he finds himself again caught by his inability to cope with uncertainty. He wishes to consult the oracles, but he has come to fear them, after what happened to his son. He decides to give the oracles a test, to determine which one he can trust. The test will take the form of the question: What is Croesus doing now? This test may be flawed, though, because it asks about the oracle's knowledge of the present, not the future, but Croesus apparently does not see the difference, and wishes to ensure that his future be as definite as the present. With his test, Croesus exercises his ability to gain scientific knowledge about the present, but gains no insight into his future. Croesus' judgment is not very sophisticated. He has trouble considering possibilities and contingencies, and would like to make his decisions based on a linear analysis he can perform on the phenomena as they are in the now.

With the false assurance he got from his test, Croesus makes the most important decision of his career in terms that repeat the mistake he made with the prophecy concerning Atys. Having received the oracle "If [Croesus] made war on the Persians he would destroy a mighty empire" (1. 53), Croesus responds with the most straightforward interpretation. Croesus interprets this prophecy from the perspective of his own intention to conquer Persia, without considering that it could equally coincide with his own destruction. Croesus does not consider all the possibilities and so "misses the meaning" of this oracle (1. 71). Through his test, Croesus thought he had guaranteed for himself a "true oracle" (1. 49). His assessment of truth and falsehood is limited because he relies on science in a case that demands the ability to interpret language dialogically, an ability that the poet John Keats called "negative capability:" the ability to acknowledge ambiguity.[18]

Croesus' deficient response to yet a third oracle further illustrates his inability to operate within a framework of uncertainty. To Croesus' third question "Will my monarchy last long?" (1. 55), the oracle responds with "whenever a mule becomes king to the Medes...flee and think not to stand fast..." (1. 55). Again, Croesus considers only the most superficial interpretation. Croesus, says Herodotus, "thought that a mule would surely never become king of the Medians instead of a man, and so neither he himself nor his issue would ever be deprived of the power" (1. 56). Croesus does not consider the possibility that the mule of the oracle is not literally a beast. The mule is a metaphor for Cyrus, a 'crossbreed' who had a Median mother and a Persian father.

To a modern reader, Croesus' neglect of the interpretive art can appear naïve, as though he can only sustain his resolve by his giving the oracle its most superficial interpretation. Although the oracle later accuses Croesus of misinterpretation ("he did not understand what was said, nor did he make question again" 1. 91), he is spared the need for remorse, for the god also admits that Croesus' freedom was illusory and limited. "Let Croesus know that his fall is three years later than the destined moment," the oracle declares later in 1. 91. The fall of Lydia is linked to crimes committed by Croesus' ancestors, which perhaps could be read as a metaphor for the long-term impact of earlier strategic and policy failures. Ulti-

---

18 Keats, John. 1817. "Letter to his brother." Web. See also Simpson, Peter and Robert French. 2006. "Negative Capability and the Capacity to Think in the Present Moment: Some Implications for Leadership Practice." *Leadership* 2.2: 245-55.

mately, Croesus' decisions operate within an environment already limited by the decisions of past rulers.

The bond to necessity can take many forms. Without discounting the role of the gods, it is evident that Croesus' plans for his invasion of Persia were limited by his own one-dimensional thinking and his inability to consider details that didn't fit within his linear interpretive model. Croesus' handicap is illustrative of a confirmation bias toward a linear truth that is stable and predictable. Such a prejudice serves as "an authoritative guide for our Western intuition, but one that is idealized and liable to mislead us when the surrounding world and its messy realities do not fit this notion."[19]

Croesus' mistaken conviction that he had provided himself with a scientific test for the predictions of oracles illustrates yet another problem: the future is difficult to work into scientific predictive models. The military theorist Clausewitz cautions against treating the information one receives in war as 'evidence': "The great part of the information obtained in War is contradictory, a still greater part is false, and by far the greatest part is of a doubtful character. What is required of an officer is a certain power of discrimination, which only knowledge of men and things and good judgment can give."[20]

Because information is ever changing, a strategist must be careful not to lapse inadvertently into the human bias for predictability and linearity:

An important basis for confusion is association of the norm not only with simplicity, but with obedience to rules and thus with expected behavior – which places blinders on our ability to see

---

19 Beyerchen, Alan. 1992. "Clausewitz, Nonlinearity and the Unpredictability of War." *International Security* 17.3: 59-90.

20 Ibid., 61.

the world around us. Nonlinear phenomena are thus usually regarded as recalcitrant misfits in our catalog of norms, although they are actually more prevalent than phenomena that conform to the rules of linearity. This can seriously distort perceptions of what is central and what is marginal – a distortion that Clausewitz as a realist understands in *On War*.[21]

Croesus' assumption that the 'great empire' he was prophesied to destroy was that of his enemy was furthered by his rhetorical inference that 'the enemy' is 'the one destined to be destroyed'. Even today, such an association can be problematic when it is equated with a one-dimensional expectation of the enemy. President George W. Bush's 2002 depiction of an "axis of evil" in the Middle East set up the expectation of a unilateral, one-dimensional opposition similar to that offered by the Axis powers during wwii, an expectation that would have to be overcome before the situation could be understood as it was.

Croesus' story has an epilogue. His story touched Cyrus, who kept him near as a *memento mori* after defeating him in battle and subjecting Lydia to the Persian Empire. While he was king, Croesus could not employ a narrative that functions within the human art of interpretation, but after his fall he is permitted discourse with the divine. Already burning on the pyre, Croesus calls to Apollo and the fire is quenched (1. 87). After his rescue from the pyre, the one favor Croesus asks of Cyrus is that he be allowed to continue his speech with the god (1. 90). As a result of this communication with Apollo, Croesus learns that divine involvement does not absolve him of responsibility. To Cyrus' question "who of all mankind persuaded

---

21 Ibid.

you to make war upon my land?" Croesus initially answers "I myself did..., but the cause of it was the god of the Greeks, who incited me to fight" (1. 87). However, Herodotus tells us that after Apollo's final words, Croesus "acknowledged that the fault had been none of the god's but his own" (1. 91).

Croesus is tragic because he has all the responsibility of reason without any of its power. His world, perhaps more like ours than we would admit, is filled with oracular messages both ambiguous and deceptive, and his fate is, at least partly, the result of incidents that took place five generations before his time. A leader must act: Croesus cannot remain passive. Ambiguous oracles demand interpretation, and in interpretation there is a space for free choice. But the freedom Croesus thinks he is exercising in his interpretation of the oracle is shown to be illusory. Herodotus describes Croesus' oracle as 'false-coin' (1. 75). Just as a counterfeit coin is made and put into circulation, so the false-coin oracle is given by gods who know that it will deceive anyone who is too literal-minded to interpret it carefully.

The story of Croesus shows that the art of interpreting complex and uncertain situations requires a linguistic perspective that goes beyond literal meaning, for the literal meaning is associated with the counterfeit. If we replace Croesus' god with science's own prejudice for clarity, which can limit the student's ability to interpret complex situations, the analogy of enslavement remains relevant.[22]

---

22 Ibid., 62: "'Nonlinear' indicates that the norm is what it negates... [Such] words are deeply rooted in a cultural heritage that stems from the classical Greeks. The underlying notion is that 'truth' resides in the simple (and thus the stable, regular, and consistent) rather than in the complex (and therefore unstable, irregular, and inconsistent). The result has been an authoritative guide for our Western intuition, but one that is idealized and liable to mislead us when the surrounding world and its messy realities do not fit this notion."

The limitations of a habitual or literal mindset are made much of in today's management and leadership textbooks. These fields have created a market for addressing this human limitation with a series of self-help approaches.[23] The message is always the same: To wield our power we must free ourselves from the blind necessities of our own linear expectations.

Herodotus goes on to describe how the Greeks fared somewhat better than Croesus in the process of developing an art of interpretation adequate to the complexities of warfare. The Spartans also once received a 'false-coin' oracle (1. 66). As the Spartans were growing stronger, they too petitioned the oracle about a hoped-for conquest. The response they received is similar to the response given to Croesus. To the Spartans, the oracle said "Tegea will I give you, to beat with your feet in dancing, and with a rope to measure, to your fill, her beautiful plainland" (1. 66). The Spartans, like Croesus made the mistake of interpreting this oracle according to their own hopes, and invaded Tegea. The defeated Spartan prisoners revealed the metaphorical meaning of the oracle as they worked the plains of Tegea in fetters.

The Spartan defeat in Tegea is not definitive. The Spartan state survives, and the Spartans go on to master the art of interpretation. By the time the Spartans encounter the false-coin oracle, they have already taken control of their own future by instituting the rule of law that still governs their state during the time of the Persian invasion. Herodotus frequently associates the rule of law with developing in its adherents a flexibility of mind and freedom of thought that Herodotus finds lacking in the subjects of totalitarian regimes.

23 Robert Cialdini labels this tendency 'The Foolish Fortress.' Cialdini, Robert. 2009. *Influence: Science and Practice*. Boston: Allyn & Bacon.

In Book One of the *History*, Herodotus seems to equate the rise of the rule of law with an improvement in the human capacity for the interpretive arts. Herodotus explains this institution of law in terms of its connection to freedom of speech. Herodotus attributes Lycurgus (the ancient and legendary figure credited with writing the constitution that would form the basis for political life in Sparta) with instituting a transformation of the Spartan character that is equated with making the Spartans more open to communication. Herodotus says,

> Before this the Spartans had been, in respect of the laws, the very worst of all the Greeks, one might say, and in their dealings with others, and also among themselves, the least free in communication. But then they changed over toward good laws… (1. 65)

Despite their new freedom of discourse, the Spartans are tricked by the false-coin oracle and invade Tegea. In the time of Croesus, however, they have a second chance to interpret an ambiguous oracle correctly, and this time they succeed.

After years of subjection, the Spartans ask the Delphic oracle "what god they should propitiate that they might win against Tegea" (1. 67). The oracle instructs them to bring home to Sparta the bones of Orestes. To a second question, asking where the bones of Orestes lay, the oracle responds ambiguously, speaking of a place in Tegea "where two winds are a-blowing" and "blow rings answer to blow" (1. 67). The Spartan Lichas solves the riddle by interpreting the oracle's words as referring to the bellows, hammer and anvil of a Tegean blacksmith.

Lichas is able to solve the riddle of the bones of Orestes partly because of what Herodotus calls "good luck and... his own cleverness (*sophia*)" (I. 68), and partly because of the new open relations between Tegea and Sparta. Herodotus notes "there was at this time free intercourse with Tegea..." (I. 68). Once the riddle is solved, the Spartans construct a scheme by which Lichas is able to persuade the Tegean smith to grant him access to the plot of land where Orestes is buried. Sparta's defeat of Tegea is linked to an ambiguous oracle, but this time there is in addition a man who succeeds in translating ambiguity into effective action through the interpretive power of language.

The Spartans learned that the art of interpretation depends upon open relations and a multicultural awareness. Strategists need exposure to diverse points of view and to evidence that may not support the dominant interpretive paradigm. As the story of Croesus cautions, this ability to think broadly and figuratively about the significance of diverse evidence is not always compatible with the forthright attitude of command. One of Herodotus' motives is to enable his people, the Greeks, to acquire a working knowledge of their enemies, the Persians, in order to better prepare their defense should the Persians attempt a third invasion. In this, the Herodotean project supports the need to provide the defense community with the material for a humanistic judgment. The Greeks were amateurs at defense when they successfully resisted the Persians. During the fifty years after their victory, the Greek city-states grew more professional about defense, and by the time the Peloponnesian War broke out, Athens and Sparta were respectively renowned for their trained, standing navy and army. Herodotus' view of a multicultural humanism at the core of defense policy was threatened by this very professionalism, a phenomenon that J. Glenn Gray explains:

> The professional is caught in a world of means and instruments, himself one among others. He makes war a means for furthering political ends, and his preoccupation like his occupation is seldom with things for their own sake. This is the abiding curse of the military profession. The total human being has no chance to break through to consciousness because there is no official interest in the whole human being.[24]

The next chapter will take up in a new context the relationship between the free art of interpretation and the acquisition of power. In Herodotus' story of Cyrus' rise and the Ionians' fall, Cyrus is fated to succeed because of his unerring ability to focus his own divergent sense of his own identity, in order to see past the simplistic labels that brand him, within his own society, as a lowly servant. With an air of inevitability, Cyrus translates his potential into actual power. In this chapter, we have seen that this ability to transform is the hallmark of rule. As Herodotus continues his description of the Persian invasions, the Greek resistance produces individuals like Themistocles, who have the aptitude for command, and yet remain subordinate to the primacy of law. Also in the next chapter, we will look at Herodotus' account of the origins of the rule of law. The rule of law requires that those who obey it speak a common language, which in turn enables a forum for men to compete non-violently for power, using only their rhetorical skill to persuade others to follow them. The forum of political persuasion returns us full-circle to the

---

24 Gray, *The Warriors*, 147-8.

human inclination toward polarizing rhetoric and starkly dualistic portrayals of self and other, rhetoric that continues to operate as though with a force of necessity on human affairs. Language has an extraordinary power to shape perception, a power that can be used for good or ill.

Chapter 4

The Power of Language

After defeating Croesus, Cyrus consolidated the Persian Empire. With Cyrus' rise, the age of fated failure appears to be over. Cyrus and his contemporaries in Greece exhibit a remarkable freedom to determine their own destinies. Croesus' literalness and one-dimensional approach to problem solving are not repeated by his successor. On the contrary, a spirit of individualism emerges across Asia Minor and Greece, tied to an increasing sense of the transformative power of language. This next generation of leaders utilize this transformative power to startling effect. The difference between these powerful individuals emerging in Asia Minor and Greece appears to be that in Asia Minor, the rule of law does not develop, whereas in Greece, the most powerful men learn how to submit themselves to the restraints of their city-states' emerging legal systems.

Cyrus' lifetime of conquest is patterned on the model of Cyrus' own transformation, from lowly shepherd to emperor. Herodotus describes Cyrus' success as fated in a certain sense, and yet Herodotus shows us how much of Cyrus' rise is owed to Cyrus' exercise of his own talents. In some ways, Croesus and Cyrus represent two sides of the same problem: how language, as the tool that formulates identity, can constitute a force of necessity in human affairs. Croesus' awareness of himself is limited by the conventional terms of tradition and prophecy; his identity is fixed and inert. Croesus takes the world at face value. Cyrus, by contrast, refuses to accept the constraints of convention, and uses language in diverse and creative ways to transcend his apparent class and status.

As Cyrus was rising in the east, the Greek city-states were producing men with similar talents for acquiring power, yet the Greeks were simultaneously learning how to restrain individual ambition with the rule of law. In Athens, the rule of law created an arena in which political power could be acquired through persuasion. The Persian tyrants after Cyrus, by contrast, turn to the methods of force and terror. In this chapter, we trace the emerging distinction that Herodotus illustrates between tyranny and the rule of law.

The king Astyages dreams that his grandson, the baby Cyrus, will usurp his kingdom. Like Croesus confronted with his dream about his son's death, Astyages would like to thwart the necessity of this prophecy. Astyages, like Croesus, can only fathom one course of action consonant with his dream. For Cyrus to remain alive is for fate to have a control which Astyages cannot endure. Astyages adopts the most literal course: he orders the murder of the baby Cyrus. In his conviction that murder is the one free act permitted him, Astyages is most deceived. Astyages' story mirrors that of Oedipus' father Laius, who is destroyed by the child he once tried to murder.[1] The baby Cyrus survives, although as a consequence of the murder attempt he is raised by a cowherd, 'dead' to aristocratic society.

---

1   Sophocles. 2013. *Oedipus the King*. In *Antigone, Oedipus the King, Oedipus at Colonus*. Edited by David Grene and Richmond Lattimore. Chicago: University of Chicago Press.

The baby who was so "big and beautiful" (1. 112) at birth grows up among animals. Despite his lowly upbringing, his royal nature emerges. At the age of ten, "the children in their play chose him for their king – him who was called the cowherd's son" (1. 114). Cyrus did not yet know of his royal birth, but he is already beginning to transcend his apparent identity as a cowherd's son.

Cyrus is naturally suited to absolute rule, a propensity that emerges when he gets in trouble for whipping an aristocrat's son who did not follow his orders:

> … the children of the village… in their play made me their king; they judged that I was the most suited to the office. All the other boys did what I bade them do, but this one was deaf to my orders and would none of them, until finally he was punished for it (1. 115).

Knowing nothing of his royal lineage, Cyrus initially sees himself as earning his rule through consensus. However, as this anecdote shows, Cyrus' early understanding of his right to rule associates his power with his willingness to use force on his subjects.

Astyages recognizes Cyrus because of the physical resemblance, and also because Cyrus' speech is not subordinate as that of a cowherd's son would be:

> The look on the boy's face seemed to [Astyages] to resemble his own and his style of answering to be too free for what he appeared to be (1. 116).

Cyrus' free use of speech reveals his true identity to the frightened Astyages. Cyrus is not restricted by his lowly position in a rigidly aristocratic society. Displaying his natural talent for conquest, he is elected king by his peers. Any democratic potential in this election is quickly suppressed as Cyrus strengthens his tyranny with shows of force. Yet alongside his taste for force, Cyrus has a growing interest in using language creatively to manipulate others' perceptions of him.

Cyrus acquired power at the grass-roots level, by persuading his peers that he is the most suited to rule. Once he has been recognized by Astyages, and his kingly identity officially established, he continues his insurgency through deception, exploiting the ambiguities of language to consolidate his power. Although he is now acknowledged as the king's lawful heir, Cyrus allows himself to be persuaded by Harpagus to overthrow Astyages. Harpagus sends a secret message to incite Cyrus to revolt:

> [Harpagus] artfully prepared a hare by slitting its belly without removing any of the fur, and he inserted into the hare, just as it was, a papyrus on which he wrote what he wanted (1. 123).

Harpagus' written argument persuades Cyrus to pursue his ambitions to take over the kingdom. Cyrus in turn persuades the Persians to follow his lead. Following Harpagus' example, Cyrus tricks the Persians by another ploy involving writing:

> He wrote what he would upon a papyrus, and called an assembly of the Persians. At this he unfolded the papyrus and read it aloud to the effect that Astyages had appointed him general of the Persians (1. 125).

Harpagus and Cyrus are able to manipulate the distinction between appearances and reality, yet Cyrus is particularly brazen in the directness with which he goes about his deception. Herodotus tells this story without recording what Cyrus wrote, implying that the content of this message was not as important as how it was presented. Cyrus gains the support of the Persians by exploiting the authority of the written word, available only to aristocrats, which impresses the common people merely by its appearance.[2] So far, Cyrus has consolidated his power by non-violent means, appealing to the people and promising them better conditions than they find under Astyages.

Cyrus rises through insurgency, in the manner of the Greek tyrants, using persuasion and promises of a better life to marshal the lowest social class to join him in revolt. Herodotus includes a parallel story about the Greek tyrant Pisistratus, who rose among the Athenians by using the name of freedom. Cyrus also appeals to the Persians' longing for freedom: "The Persians had their champion now and were glad to free themselves" (1. 127). This freedom, however, does not imply that individuals would have a voice in their government. Cyrus does not experiment with democracy; he defines freedom as national sovereignty with one-man rule.

Cyrus' sense of himself as an individual not defined by his apparent class identity gives him an autonomy that stands out in Herodotus' account of the early history of Asia Minor, the region we know now as the Middle East. Cyrus consolidates the power

---

2   In Book Eight, Themistocles paints onto rocks facing the sea messages urging the Ionians in Xerxes' army to revolt, knowing that, even if the messages do not persuade the Ionians, they will weaken Xerxes' army by diminishing Xerxes' trust in his Greek troops (8. 22).

to overthrow Astyages by working at the grass-roots level with an appeal to the Persians' desire for a better quality of life. Free-minded and flexible, Cyrus has not settled into the complacency that defines the later tyrant Xerxes, who led the second Persian invasion of Greece. The stories that Herodotus tells of Xerxes stereotype him as a complacent tyrant, who has lost the manly virtues. Herodotus' portrayal of Cyrus, the founder of the Persian Empire, challenges this stereotype of tyranny by showing us a man with the natural ability to acquire rule.

Many of the stories Herodotus tells are characteristic of what we would call insurgency. Insurgencies are political revolts. The story of Cyrus is the story of a grass-roots insurgency, as Cyrus successfully mobilizes the Persians to support his bid for absolute rule. Grass-roots insurgency is a particular phenomenon that deserves careful attention. Campaigns that mobilize the masses demonstrate a unique type of leadership and strategy, that goes beyond a coup, an overthrow by force alone. According to Herodotus, Cyrus was not the first in his family to demonstrate a capacity for grass-roots insurgency. Cyrus' great-great-grandfather Deioces provides another prototype of a successful insurgency. Deioces uses grass-roots judicial techniques to make himself indispensable to the people:

> At the time, the Medes lived in villages, and in the particular village of Deioces he had always been a man of note, and now he set himself to practice justice ever more and more keenly. There was at the time great lawlessness throughout Media, and Deioces did what he did because he knew that injustice is the great enemy of justice. The Medes in his own village, seeing the manner of the man's life, chose him to be a judge among

them. And he, since it was power that he was courting, was always straight and just and, for being so, won no small praise from his fellow citizens – so much so, indeed, that the people in other villages learned that Deioces was the one man for judging according to the rule of right; these people had before met with unjust sentences, and when they heard the good news about Deioces they flocked to him to have their own cases decided by him; and at last they would entrust their suits to none but him (1. 96)

When Deioces had consolidated the power he had acquired by settling disputes and handing out justice in the villages, he uses his leverage with the people to seize power at the government level:

Deioces came to realize that now everything hung upon himself. Whereupon he refused to sit as judge anymore and said that he would serve no longer. It did not profit him at all, he said, to decide cases for his neighbors all day long to the manifest neglect of his own affairs. So robbery and lawlessness grew even more in the villages than before. The Medes all came to a meeting place and conferred… What they said was, "If we go on as we are going now, we will not be able to live in this country at all. Let us therefore set up a king over us…" Then at once the question was proposed as to whom to make king. Deioces was so much in everyone's mouth, people both putting him forward and praising him, that all ended by agreeing that he should be their king. For his part, he bade them build him houses worthy of royalty and to strengthen him with a bodyguard (1. 97-98)

Deioces' usurpation of Media is a prototypical insurgency, gaining power initially not by force, but through an appeal to the peoples' desire for a better life, through improvements in governance, security, economic and moral order. This is how the Taliban came to power in Afghanistan, by mediating and resolving disputes at the local level, by providing security, and by stimulating the local economies with the poppy crop.[3] Deioces' story also illustrates the way such movements become living systems, for once begun, Deioces' plan continues forward in the political council without his presence, just as do successful insurgencies in our age.[4]

Deioces did not follow up his interest in the judicial process by establishing the rule of law, but instead withdrew from the people's presence in order to begin a rule of terror. Once the people had fortified his palaces and equipped him with bodyguards, Deioces withdraws: "When all was built, Deioces was the first who established this ceremony; that no one whatsoever should have admittance to the king" (1. 99). Fearing competition, Deioces introduced elaborate rituals to govern his subjects' interactions with him, "so that those who were his equals and of the same age, brought up with him, and of descent as good, and as brave as he, might not, seeing him, be vexed and take to plotting against him" (1. 99).

Deioces' great-great-grandson Cyrus similarly acquires power through his creative use of language, yet in his absolute rule he denies this opportunity to others. The Persians traditionally valued telling the truth as a martial virtue, a mark of a man who loves honor. Prior to Cyrus' consolidation of power, the Persians appear to

---

3   Kilcullen, David. 2010. *Counterinsurgency*. Oxford: Oxford University Press, 157.

4   Ibid, 194.

have had an honor code, similar to the martial honor code in Sparta, where nobility was defined by martial prowess and personal integrity. Martial prowess was displayed through excellence at horseback riding and archery; personal integrity by a straightforward appreciation of the truth: "Lying is considered among them the very basest thing" (1. 138). At the time Cyrus led them to revolt and seize the empire, the Persians had in place many of the same customs that in Sparta came to political fruition in a martial constitution. Cyrus manipulates these customs in order to perpetrate his own power. Cyrus has no need for a political language, and he has no interest in fostering a political community among his people.

In Herodotus' account, Cyrus envisions a type of tyranny that acquires, over time, an abstract power of its own, a power that inevitably drains virility from its subjects. Herodotus makes the point that the Persians' virility declined as a result of the methods of terror employed by Xerxes. Watching his best troops mowed down by the 300 Spartans attempting to hold the pass at Thermopylae, Xerxes comes to see for himself how impotent are his men. Punning on the two Greek words for men: *androi*, which is associated with the male virtues of virility and strength, and *anthropoi*, a more generic term that refers to all humans, Herodotus describes Xerxes' realization that although he commands many male humans, he has few real men (7. 210).

Herodotus offers the Greek character Pisistratus as a different type of leader of insurgency. Pisistratus has many of the same character traits as Cyrus, but is influenced as well by the Greek democratic spirit and growing respect for the rule of law. The Greek tyrant Pisistratus initially tried to use his power to preserve the laws.

Pisistratus seized power using methods similar to those employed by Cyrus, yet he left existing legislative processes in place:

> Pisistratus took over the power in Athens; yet he in no way deranged the existing magistracies or the ordinances but governed the city well and truly according to the laws that were established (1. 59).

At some point, Pisistratus could not maintain both the rule of law and his own position, and he eventually becomes a tyrant as arbitrary as Cyrus. At the time of Cyrus, Athens also was ruled by force, and did not return to the rule of law until shortly before the first Persian invasion, in 507 BCE (see 5. 55). The stories of Deioces and Cyrus in Persia, and Pisistratus in Greece, show that some means of addressing local concerns about justice, security, and economic welfare are essential for consolidating one-man rule through an appeal to the people. Once in power, however, the Persian kings and Greek tyrants eliminate democratic processes and dispense their own justice.

From these men's stories, the questions arise: How might a spirited, ambitious personality be persuaded to adopt the self-imposed limitations of voluntary submission to the rule of law? How does one found a democracy? For Herodotus, the Athenian lawgiver Solon is the paradigmatic founder of democracy, the founder who understands that his primary mission is to enable democracy as a living system, one in which processes thrive without autocratic oversight. In America, George Washington similarly understood that his hardest and yet most imperative task was to step down and let another take the highest office in the land.[5]

A commitment to the rule of law need not limit a leader's inventiveness, but it can insert a potent and fertile tension between ambition and self-imposed, principled restraint. Herodotus depicts Cyrus and Deioces as characters who lacked this restraint. Cyrus and Deioces are each ruthless and smart, capable of stratagems whose means we must admire even if we can't condone their ends. These are men of action who are as intelligent as they are bold. They appear as very modern characters, displaying a compelling combination of audacity, nerve, and self-control that we associate with many of our own most successful leaders.

Herodotus suggests that the difference between tyranny and democracy is not in the opportunities each gives the individual to acquire power and influence, but in how the individual chooses to govern once in power. The acquisition of power depends on individuals with a strong entrepreneurial spirit and a sense of their own autonomy. Yet the rule of law encourages participation in the political process through non-violent competition, while tyranny turns to force and terror to eliminate competition.

Herodotus understands that the story of the Persian invasion begins with the story of how both Asia Minor and Greece learned to consolidate their powers, through their acquiring a strong sense of the individual and the power of a single individual to affect human affairs. As we saw in the last chapter, Sparta emerged as a powerful nation-state only when it was able to produce individuals, like Lichas, who were free enough in their self-understanding to

5   See Brookhiser, Richard. 1997. *Founding Father: Rediscovering George Washington*. New York: Free Press.

use speech creatively for their own ends. At the same time, a similar individualism was emerging in the east. The difference between the two regions was in their willingness to codify their practices into universal terms that have a collective benefit in mind.

Despite his admitted fascination with the stories of Deioces, Cyrus, and Pisistratus, Herodotus expresses his ideological preference for the rule of law, which does not terrify its subjects and limit their potential, but seeks instead to strengthen them in spirit and in reason by introducing an arena for non-violent, political competition. The rule of law allows human power to develop within the social unit through a common discourse. The exercise of constitutional power can go beyond imparting justice, it can foster love of honor when those in power have speech with those they hope to influence. In a comment about the Spartans, Herodotus suggests that the only tyranny that enables men to become excellent is the power of law: "So it is with the Lacedaemonians; fighting singly, they are no worse than any other people; together, they are the most gallant men on earth. For they are free – but not altogether so. They have as despot over them Law, and they fear him" (7. 104).

In his depiction of the political trajectories taken by Asia Minor and Greece, Herodotus documents the emergence in Greece of a rule of law that would hold aspiring tyrants in check. In Book One, we meet the two great Greek lawgivers, Solon and Lycurgus. Although these men's stories have acquired some mythical elements, Herodotus dismisses any suggestion that they are divinities, preferring instead to establish their political insights as rooted in human wisdom. Herodotus tells a legend about the Delphic oracle's addressing Lycurgus as a god. As Lycurgus, approached, the oracle said "I ask myself whether as a god or a man I shall hail you. Nay but 'tis rather a god that I see in you, Lycurgus" (1. 65). Herodotus reinterprets this as a metaphor, as the oracle's musing over how properly to address such an exalted man. In Herodotus' view, unless the lawgivers are human, their institution will not be within human control. Similarly, Herodotus shows forth Solon's humanity by noting that the Athenians chose both the rule of law and Solon their lawgiver. Lawgivers should never be mistaken for gods. Their work is to bring autonomy to the human sphere, by replacing long-standing customs and traditions that do not serve human ends.

In Greece, before there could be any hope of a widespread adoption of the rule of law, individuals needed a mechanism for acquiring power freely within their social units, and these social units needed national mechanisms for interacting with other city-states, whose aid they would depend on for defense. These mechanisms required new forms of speech, developed by those who understood that language has the power to transform men and nations. Cyrus fulfilled his tyrannical destiny through a personal transformation effected by language, and it is with Cyrus that the Persian threat to Greece becomes imperative. When Cyrus appears in all his strength, the Greek power is still nascent and unformed. The Greeks need to transform themselves in a manner similar to Cyrus. Unlike Croesus and Cyrus, however, the outcome of their transformation is not prophesied. The Greeks are free to fail.

The story of the Greek transformation is, like that of Persia, a grass-roots story. For the Greeks, this begins at the level of shared language. From the first, Herodotus attributes Greek power to the common Greek language:

> But the Greek stock, since ever it was, has always used the Greek language, in my judgment. But though it was weak when it split off from the Pelasgians, it has grown from something small to be a multitude of peoples by the accretion chiefly of the Pelasgians but of many other barbarian peoples as well. But before that, it seems to me, the Pelasgian people, so long as it spoke a language other than Greek, never grew great anywhere (1. 58).

In Herodotus' opinion, the cohesion of power depends on the use of a common language. The Greeks comprise a number of different races, whose origins and assimilation have long since faded. The Greek language has exceptional political potential, it is shared by different cultures and races. As a political language, Greek unites the people who use it, and establishes the Hellenic world as a social and political unit that transcends the narrower tribal and cultural boundaries of the city-states.

Herodotus' story in Book One of the fall of Ionia sets the model for how he will assess the more encompassing story of the Greek power emerging on the mainland. The Ionians, clustered off the coast of Asia Minor, are isolated geographically by their distance from mainland Greece and by their numerous islands. When we first encounter the Ionians in Herodotus' narrative, the individual islands operate out of self-interest, and unite only occasionally. Comprising both autonomous and subject city-states, they make and break alliances with the Persian tyrants as best they can. When Herodotus first looks at the Ionians, they are indistinguishable from other groups struggling to survive the Persian threat. But their use of the Greek language soon makes their story of central concern.

Most of the Ionian island-states are consumed by their minor ethnic distinctions, in particular their dialectical differences. "These people," Herodotus writes, "do not all use the same speech; there are in fact four dialects" (1. 142). Despite their different dialects, twelve cities of Ionians have established something called the Panionium, the All-Ionian council, a political and religious meeting place. Herodotus gives the history of the Panionium as follows:

> These Ionians of the Twelve Cities are distinguished from the rest of the Ionians for one reason only, and I shall tell it. At this time, the whole Hellenic race was weak, and far the weakest of all its constituent nations, and of the least note, were the Ionians. Indeed, except for Athens, they had no city of consequence. The other Ionians, and the Athenians too, shunned the name, not wishing to be called Ionians. Even now, it seems to me, they are ashamed by the name. These twelve cities, however, took pride in the name and set up a holy place of their own, to which they gave the title Panionium (1. 143).

The twelve cities of the Panionium are remarkable because they set aside their individual lineages. Herodotus says of them, "[they] set more store by the name Ionian than all the other Ionians" (1. 147). However, while pride in their name is necessary for political unity, it is not sufficient for political strength. Upon forming the holy Panionium, their first thought is how to keep others out. Herodotus notes that "they took a resolution not share this [holy place] with any other Ionians" (1. 143).

The story of the Ionians illustrates what academic journalist Michael Ignatieff terms "the narcissism of minor difference."[6] In his report of the war that ripped apart Bosnia and Herzegovina in the early 1990's, Ignatieff tells how Serbs and Croats, once neighbors and friends, transformed into enemies. Ignatieff is interested in how it can be that "people who once had a lot in common end up having nothing in common but war." From his perspective as a reporter traveling through Bosnia during the war years, Ignatieff did not see evidence of any deep seated cultural 'fault lines' that would point to the inevitability of war. On the contrary, Ignatieff finds the apparent ideological metaphors to be inadequate to explain the split:

> These metaphors take for granted what needs to be explained: how neighbors once ignorant of the very idea that they belong to opposed civilizations begin to think – and hate – in these terms; how they vilify and demonize people they once called friends; how, in short, the seeds of mutual paranoia are sown, grain by grain on the soil of common life.

Ignatieff documents the emptiness of the nationalist ideologies that sprang up to justify and feed the conflict between two peoples whose lifestyles were similar and whose differences were trivial. He interviews Serbian and Croatian soldiers and concludes that the average soldier on both sides could not account for why he was at war. "The black-toqued ethnic paramilitaries may be true believers, but ordinary people – the foot soldiers of ethnic war like him – dimly, sometimes agonizingly, perceive the gap between what they see with their own eyes and what they are told to believe."

6 All quotes from Ignatieff, Michael. 1998. *The Warrior's Honor: Ethnic War and the Modern Conscience*. New York: Holt Paperbacks, 34-71.

The linguistic differences between Serbs and Croats were minor: "There are differences… in their family names, but these differences are nearly invisible to outsiders." The two peoples are of the same racial stock. Josep Broz Tito (1892-1980), wielding power tyrannically first as Prime Minister and then President of Yugoslavia, had held these two peoples together under united rule for 37 years by repressing ethnic difference: "Many Yugoslavs of the 1960s and 1970s sincerely thought they had put ethnic hatred behind them." In Bosnia and Herzegovina, it was when they were freed from Tito's tyranny that the Serbs and Croats lost their long-standing tolerance and fell to killing each other in the name of their minor ethnic distinctions.

In Herodotus' account, the Ionian island states seem similarly to magnify their minor differences, prove unable to unite into a significant opposition to Cyrus' growing power, and are quickly conquered by Cyrus because they are divided. Had they been able to unite, Herodotus tells us, "[they would have] been the most fortunate of all the Greeks" (I. 170). Herodotus believes this was a real possibility. Even conquered by the Medes, the Ionians had ships of their own and could have sailed away. In the Panionium council, one man urged this course of unity: "Bias bade the Ionians set sail and go to Sardinia, in a common enterprise, and there establish one city of all the Ionians" (I. 170). Even in their distress, the Ionian islanders had the opportunity to escape their bondage. Had Bias been more persuasive, they could have addressed the problem of their isolation.

Herodotus' view of this connection between weakness and linguistic isolation emerges even more clearly when he discusses the

Carians. Although powerful in the legendary time of their alliance with King Minos ("the Carian race was the most regarded of all at that time…" 1. 171), the Carians have grown isolated. The Carians of Herodotus' day have chosen to emphasize their obscure racial connections to the remote peoples of Lydia and Mysia: "Lydus and Mys, say the Carians, were brothers to Car" (1. 171). As a result, the Carians ignore their linguistic connections: "even those who speak the same language as the Carians are not admitted if they are of another national origins" (1. 171). The fall of the Carians to Cyrus' growing empire is tragic but unremarkable: "The Carians, then, were enslaved by Harpagus, having achieved no gallant deed at all" (1. 174).

Once the isolated islands off the coast of Asia Minor have missed the opportunity to unite, they join the rest of Asia in finding power only in resistance. The Ionians who choose slavery rather than resistance to the death will have to join in the invasion of Greece. All that their speaking Greek will gain them politically is the chance to be less useful to Persia insofar as they are less trusted.

Bias gave the Ionians good advice when he urged them to found a common country, but he was not persuasive. Herodotus presents the political use of language for persuasion as a characteristically Greek phenomenon. Cyrus dismisses the Spartans once he learns they do business in a public arena. "I never feared men," Cyrus announces, "who have a place set apart in the midst of their cities where they gather to cheat one another and exchange oaths, which they break" (1. 153). The Athenians and the Spartans, however, are able to conduct public as well as private business in the marketplace.

When power is shared, persuasion is a tool as much for politicians as merchants.

Cyrus, although he employed persuasion to seize power, does not see any advantage in politicizing its practice once he has established his authority. As we have seen, the Persians were not subtle in their approach to language and meaning. Children were taught from an early age not to employ language for any deceit: "They train their sons, from their fifth to their twentieth year in... truth-telling" (1. 136). Persian society puts great value on truth. The Persians set limits on their forms of expression, and value a language free from confusion. Although in these respects Persian culture fosters philosophy, its understanding of warfare is linear: "multitude, they think, is strength" (1. 135).

In mainland Greece, according to Herodotus, the consolidation of political power and national identity is accompanied by the growing art of persuasion. Individuals profit by understanding that language can be ambiguous. Persuasion operates by influence, not force. An interest in the powers of persuasion and influence are present in Persia, as witnessed by Cyrus' and Darius' rise to power, but once these men have acquired the kingship, they turn to force. The Athenians and Spartans, still acquiring their power, establish a political arena in which people can speak freely in the hopes of influencing one another.

The political art of persuasion requires a public arena where men can compete for each other's estimation. Herodotus acknowledges that such a political arena fosters deception: "it seems that it is easier to fool many men than one" (5. 97). The Athenians do not attempt to eliminate stratagem and the exploitation of appearances from the political process. Any Athenian can compete in the political arena with the same techniques that he can employ in the marketplace for his own private gain.

In their love of the contest, the Greeks find a political activity that is supported by the wisdom Croesus took from Solon, that "all human matters are a wheel" (1. 207). The Greeks, as the Arcadians tell Xerxes, "contend… purely for the sake of excelling" (8. 26). When political discourse is an arena of competition, an individual can fail and still return to try again. The rule of law ensures that the Greeks do not risk their lives when they stand for office. Failure entails loss of influence, which need not, like death, be a permanent condition. Poor judgment is tolerated, although not rewarded. In the Persian Empire, by contrast, individuals are rewarded or punished for their public successes and failures at the will of the king. A person who chooses public activity risks the punishment of death, sure to put a permanent end to his career (see 7. 35; 8. 65; 8. 90). In Persia, where poor judgment can mean execution, Solon's wisdom argues against a life of political activity (see 7. 18).

Herodotus puts value on human beings learning from their mistakes. Failures can teach as much, or more, as success. Herodotus says, "since, then, I know that man's good fortune never abides in the same place, I will make mention of both [great and small] alike" (1. 5). This view honors the attempt more than the outcome, and values the narratives of the failures and successes alike for what others can learn from them.

Herodotus' stories about the Athenians show them making their own attempts to resist the Persian invasions. In their response to an oracle urging them to flee their doomed city, the Athenians show a daring spirit. Refusing to accept the oracle's command that the Athenians abandon their city, they return to Delphi and demand of Apollo "a better oracle." The new oracle advises them to put their trust in "a wall of wood" (7. 141). Some Athenians interpreted this oracle, rather literally, as referring to the Acropolis, and advised barricading themselves into Athens' stronghold. Themistocles found an interpretation that aligned this oracle with his own strategic vision, and persuaded the Athenians "to prepare for a fight at sea, since the ships were their wooden wall" (7. 143). Herodotus gives the Athenians enormous credit for seeing past the most literal interpretations of the oracles they receive. The strongest opinion Herodotus expresses in the *History* is in support of this Athenian quality:

> At this point I am forced to declare an opinion that most people will find offensive; yet, because I think it true, I will not hold back. If the Athenians had taken fright at the approaching danger and had left their own country… no one would have tried to oppose the King at sea… Not even the dreadful oracles that came from Delphi, terrifying though they were, persuaded them to desert Greece (7. 139).

The Athenians wish to align their irrational faith in oracles with their sense of their own autonomy, and Themistocles shows them a good way to do this. A large factor in this is the Athenians' ability to forge a sufficient alliance with their Greek-speaking neighbors.

The political arena that, as we saw, failed to develop among the Ionians came to fruition in mainland Greece. In order to share a political forum, the city-states must share a common language. Herodotus' Athenians speak of their connection with Sparta as a linguistic connection: "there is our common Greekness; we are one in blood and one in language" (8. 144). It is true that the Athenians and the Spartans now share a common language and can communicate openly. But Athens and Sparta did not always share a common language. In fact, the Athenians have misrepresented their "common Greekness" in order to further their own interests in a national identity for Greece. These two city-states are not "one in blood." "The Athenians," Herodotus tells us, "… were themselves Pelasgians… but they changed their name again to Athenians" (8. 44). Herodotus also documents how the Pelasgian people switched over to the Greek language (1. 58). The Athenians succeeded in transforming themselves through cultivating a language in common with their mainland neighbors.

The "common Greekness" shared by Athens and Sparta is based on a common language more than a common culture. The two city-states differ in their customs and political visions, and can agree on very little. In practice, however, agreement is not as important as is the arena of discourse, which fosters competition for political influence as well as military excellence. At the time of the Persian Wars, the Athenians and Spartans are free to lie, contrive and persuade. They exercise free choice about how to interpret the oracles and develop their own strategies for military success. This unrestricted understanding of language secured the mainland Greeks' independence from conquest, just as it secured the Persian Empire for Cyrus. Like the story of Cyrus, however, the stories of Athens and Sparta go on to suggest that these states also cannot maintain the freedom of discourse once their power is assured.

Herodotus presents discourse as a political and social activity, but not as the basis for an intellectual life. With a few exceptions (Solon, for example), Herodotus' characters are not contemplative. They are active men, and they treat language as a means to power. What about Herodotus himself? As a historian, does he see a higher intellectual purpose in his own narrative? Only a few years later, Thucydides clearly viewed the composition of history as an endeavor done in the name of reason, for the sake of bringing order and insight to the apparent chaos of the real world. Did Herodotus share in his successor's vision for a rational history? For Thucydides, as also for the Greek philosophers Plato and Aristotle, narrative has an ethical backdrop in the form of the implicit question: What is right action? Herodotus resists judgment on many issues; he revels in different cultures' diverse approaches to the good. His stated mission is to show rather than to instruct, and his history has the function of an exhibition. This respect for diversity brings with it an admiration for those institutions that foster tolerance and innovation. Herodotus places positive value on the rule of law, diplomatic discourse, human autonomy, and a political process that values individual talent.

Herodotus' pragmatic and realistic approach to power remains relevant to our own democratic processes in the United States, where persuasion is a powerful tool in both politics and business. Thanks to the First Amendment to the U.S. Constitution, our public discourse is remarkably free from restrictions on its forms. The freedoms of speech delivered by the First Amendment create an environment where language functions as a human instrument, in the pursuit of human ends. Herodotus shows us a classical model in the Greeks, who also had very few restrictions on speech. Toward the end of the 5th century BCE, the unrestricted power of language was embraced by sophists such as Gorgias because of this very lack of restriction. Such sophists capitalized on speech's potential for persuading others to act against their best interests. This feature of the sophistic movement angered philosophers such as Plato, who argued in his *Republic* that unrestricted language is bestial, and that language that did not aim explicitly at truth should be censored. Even Herodotus' direct successor, Thucydides, would impose rational restrictions on the full freedom of human speech. Herodotus, by contrast, is much more at home in a multicultural environment in which customs and modes of operating can differ widely from one group to the next. In this environment, the common human element is the desire to acquire power, by whatever means possible. One might say, this is the real world.

In the next chapter, we will see the results of Athens' unrestricted democratic processes over the decades after the Persian Wars. Thucydides chronicles the Peloponnesian War, that unfolded over the last decades of the 5th century BCE. While Herodotus depicts the art of persuasion as the key to acquiring power, he gives little hint of what happened once the fledgling nation of Greece had proved its strength by resisting the Persian invasions. For the Athenians, much of the creative potential of this political form will be lost to the corrupting influence of the passions, once their great statesman Pericles (circa 495-429 BCE) dies and Athens is left without a strong minister to insist on a collective focus on the common good. As the Athenians grew more tyrannical abroad, their decision-making process at home grows more and more susceptible to their passions.

Political processes that had, under Pericles, been organized around legitimate argument and dialogue became more susceptible to the wild appetites of mobs incited by demagogues. As the American statesman James Madison (1751-1836) put it in *Federalist 55*: "Had every Athenian citizen been a Socrates, every Athenian assembly would still have been a mob."[7]

---

7   Madison, *Federalist*, 288.

Chapter 5

From Democracy to Tyranny

Fifty years after the Persian Wars that Herodotus describes, the Peloponnesian War broke out between Sparta and Athens. This war is documented by Thucydides (circa 460 – 400 BCE), whose understanding of history differs significantly from that of Herodotus. Thucydides placed great importance on the role of reason in historiography, and he discredited Herodotus' tendency to report cultural lore. For Thucydides, the historian's truth was a unitary perspective that the rigorous historian could extract from his sources through the application of logic and rigorous standards for plausibility. While this methodology implies a certain amount of oversimplification and the frequent imposition of the historian's point of view, Thucydides avoids dogmatism by his insightful portrayal of the complex and shifting dynamics of power during the Peloponnesian War, as Athenian democracy at home shifted incrementally yet inexorably into tyranny abroad, and public affairs became more and more characterized by moral relativism. In the previous two chapters, we saw how Herodotus portrays tyranny and freedom as states with overlapping human qualities. In this chapter, we will look at Thucydides' portrayal of how the Athenians' difficulties managing their fractious empire forced them to grow increasingly tyrannical abroad while simultaneously losing the integrity of their internal democratic institutions.

Throughout his *History of the Peloponnesian War*, Thucydides uses irony to illustrate the growing gap between Athens' democratic rhetoric and the reality of her tyrannical behavior. Perhaps nowhere in Thucydides is this irony more apparent than in the so-called Melian Dialogue in Book Five of the *History*, the philosophical showdown between Athens and Melos that illustrates the extent to which the Athenians had forsaken in their foreign policy their founding ideals of democracy and freedom. The Melian Dialogue, and Thucydides' subsequent account of the ill-fated Sicilian Expedition, have been read over the last few decades against the parallel backdrop of the United States's ill-fated wars in Vietnam and Iraq.[1]

Although the Peloponnesian War started as a conflict between Athens and Sparta, each side drew its allies into the war, making the conflict essentially a world war, which Thucydides describes unapologetically as "the greatest movement yet known in history" (Lattimore 1. 1).[2] Despite the pressure to take sides, two small island states in the Cyclades managed for the first 16 years of the war to remain neutral. These two were Thera (the modern Santorini) and Melos.

This neutrality was problematic for Athens. In the years after the Persian Wars, Athens gained control of the treasury of the Delian League, a defensive league of states that had formed to construct a naval defense against the possibility of another Persian invasion. Allowing small states to contribute funds rather than ships, the Athenians developed an imperial naval power of their own, and they

---

1   See Hill, *Grand Strategies*, 23-4.
2   Translations will be attributed individually by book and paragraph number, from Strassler, Robert. 1998. *The Landmark Thucydides: A Comprehensive Guide to the Peloponnesian War*. New York: Free Press; or Thucydides. 1998. *The Peloponnesian War*. Translated by Steven Lattimore. Indianapolis: Hackett Press.

used it to keep the tribute flowing from their increasingly rebellious allies. The existence of neutral states like Thera and Melos, which neither paid tribute to Athens nor were required by Sparta to install a pro-Spartan oligarchy, added incentive for Athens' own allies to revolt.

Athens managed her empire with deterrence. Revolts were punished swiftly with brutal force intended to deter other states from their own revolts. From Thucydides' account in Book Three of the Athenian debate over the fate of rebellious Mytilene, we learn that it was common practice for the Athenian military to kill all the rebelling males and enslave the women and children.

Even today, the theory of deterrence is simple: it assumes that a potential actor will be deterred by a threat that reduces the benefits and raises the costs of the action. Simple in theory, deterrence in action is a problematic strategy that rarely works as unilaterally as its theory would predict.[3] Since the Cold War ended between the United States and the former Soviet Union, deterrence has been increasingly criticized both as a theory and a strategy.[4] The basic assumptions of deterrence theory have failed repeatedly to work in practice in a variety of small-scale scenarios, and even the successful nuclear deterrence of the Cold War has been criticized on the grounds that it incites violence on a smaller scale.[5]

3   Stein, Janice. 2009. "Rational Deterrence against "Irrational" Adversaries." In *Complex Deterrence: Strategy in the Global Age*. Edited by T. V. Paul, Patrick Morgan, and James Wirtz. Chicago: University of Chicago Press, 62.

4   Paul, T. V.. "Complex Deterrence: an Introduction," In *Complex Deterrence*, 1. Also, for example, Payne, Keith. 2001. *The Fallacies of Cold War Deterrence and a New Direction*. Lexington: University Press of Kentucky.

5   For example, George, Alexander and Richard Smoke. 1974. *Deterrence in American Foreign Policy*. New York: Columbia University Press; and Jervis, Robert, Lebow, Richard Ned, and Janice Gross Stein. 1989. *Psychology and Deterrence*. Baltimore: Johns Hopkins University Press.

Independent of questions about its efficacy, deterrence raises ethical issues. If the acts it threatens are wrong, the moral question arises whether the threat itself is wrong. The philosopher Thomas Nagel sums the moral question up succinctly:

> If it is not allowable to do certain things, such as killing unarmed prisoners or civilians, then no argument about what will happen if one doesn't do them can show that doing them would be all right.[6]

It is possible that deterrence only appears moral in comparison with the acts that the deterring nation hopes not to have to do. Speaking of nuclear deterrence, military ethicist Michael Walzer writes: "We threaten evil in order not to do it, and the doing of it would be so terrible that the threat seems in comparison to be morally defensible."[7] Deterrence is a simple theory with complex applications. In the post-Cold War environment, deterrence has become a strategy applied to larger numbers of aggressive actors, with a wider diversity of motivations for their behavior, in a global framework in which power relationships are constantly shifting and unfamiliar.[8]

Thucydides' Melian Dialogue gives interesting context for the problems with deterrence strategy. This section of Thucydides' *History* is a dialogue documenting the Athenians' failed attempt to use the threat of force to compel the Melians to surrender their neutrality without a fight. In today's terminology, this is compel-

---

6   Nagel, Thomas. 1987. "War and Massacre." In *Moral Philosophy: Selected Reading*. Edited by George Shor. San Diego: Harcourt Brace Jovanovich, 670.

7   Walzer, Michael. 1977. *Just and Unjust Wars*, 4th edition. New York: Basic Books, 274.

8   Stein, *Complex Deterrence*, 59.

lance, or coercive diplomacy, rather than deterrence, but the dialogue has the clear backdrop of the Athenians' self-admitted policy of attempting deterrence to maintain the allegiance of their allies. At the end of the dialogue, the Melians choose to risk death rather than forego their honor, a choice the Athenians claim not to understand. This claim is unconvincing, and the overly reductive rhetoric in which it is framed damages the Athenian cause by strengthening the Melians in their resolve to resist.

The Melians are inflamed by the Athenian generals' dismissal of their points of honor. The Athenian generals' insistence that matters of defense should only involve realist material considerations defeats the diplomatic potential of this exchange. In adhering to a strategy of strict realism, the Athenian generals overlook psychological components that end up being critical determinants of the Melians' decision to reject the Athenians' terms.

The Case of Melos

In 416 BCE, an Athenian expedition led by the generals Cleomedes and Tisias arrived at the neutral island of Melos and attempted to compel it to surrender with the threat of overwhelming force. Although the Athenians frequently used a show of force to deter their allies from revolt and compel their enemies to obey (1. 46-51; 1.99; 3. 1-35), this is the first instance in Thucydides' *History* of a city-state using the threat of force to compel a neutral to surrender unconditionally (cf. 2. 72; 3. 68).

Melos was strategically significant – it is in the middle of the Cyclades and on the trade route from Athens to Crete and Asia

Minor (8. 39). It has a secure natural harbor. We learn in 2.9 that Melos and Thera are the only two islands in the Cyclades that have had any success resisting the Athenian Empire. Melos' resistance has been strong: in 3.91 we read of an unsuccessful Athenian expedition led by the general Nicias against Melos in 426 BCE. A Spartan colony, Melos has maintained its neutrality, although in the face of Athenian hostility it has developed a closer friendship with Sparta.

In order to understand both the security problem that Melos represents for Athens in 416 BCE and the limitations of the Athenian approach to this problem, we will first compare the Melian situation to another Athenian attempt at deterrence in 432 BCE, an effort to delay or prevent the outbreak of war. This attempt was also unsuccessful and, like the Melian situation, involved clear provocations on Athens' part. Nonetheless, the diplomatic language of the two attempts differ in some important ways. This difference in diplomatic rhetoric is corroborated by evidence elsewhere in Thucydides that Athens' management of her empire shifted significantly between 432 and 416 BCE. This shift was due to increasing rebellions among Athens' tribute-bearing allies, rebellions which required Athens to commit its resources to defending itself against its own so-called allies, leaving it desperate for some offensive strategy, some effective deterrent, that will forestall such rebellions before they begin. The unsuccessful search for an effective deterrent results in the escalation of Athenian aggression that occurs at Melos. In documenting this shift in the Athenians' foreign policy, we will borrow some terminology from Plato's *Republic* in order to understand how and why the Athenians came to be increasingly driven in their policy decisions by fear. Finally, we will analyze the Melian Dialogue itself to see the problems with this ineffective Athenian strategy and, in particular, to learn why the Athenians fail to compel the Melians to surrender despite the credibility of their threat of force. This section too will borrow some of Plato's language to illustrate the role that spirit and honor play in the Melian choice to resist.

In all of Thucydides' examples of deterrence, even those attempted by non-Athenian actors, the attempt itself is provocative in that it arouses in the target an irrational passion for resistance. Thucydides himself accounts for this possibility, for while he draws attention to the "enormous significance" of the motives of expediency and self-interest, he frequently depicts states acting irrationally.[9] The irrational political motives that operate in Thucydides' *History* are actually quite explicable, especially when mapped onto Plato's account of the appetite and the spirit, the two irrational components of Plato's tripartite soul.

The Outbreak of War

Apart from the Melian affair, Thucydides includes several other examples of the attempt to compel with the threat of force, all during the escalation of tension just prior to the outbreak of the Peloponnesian War.[10] Thucydides links all of these earlier 'cold war' attempts to the outbreak of the Peloponnesian War. Taken together, these other cases suggest that we should be skeptical about the Athenians' strategy even before reading the Melian Dialogue.

---

9   Zagorin, Peter. 2005. *Thucydides: An Introduction for the Common Reader.* Princeton: Princeton University Press,143-46.
10 Lebow, Richard Ned. 2007. "Thucydides and Deterrence." *Security Studies* 16.2: 166-167.

These earlier instances comprise some of the events that constitute for Thucydides the openly expressed causes of the Peloponnesian War.[11] The Greek city-states of Corcyra and Corinth are responsible for several of these examples during the events leading up to open battle between them. Corcyra, an island off of Greece's west coast, had formed an alliance with Athens just before the war. Corinth, the city-state on the isthmus that separates mainland Greece from the Peloponnese, was a Spartan ally. The two cities were hostile because Corcyra had resisted Spartan political control, despite being originally a Spartan colony. In the Corcyran episode, both Corcyra and Corinth attempt to compel each other with threats at a time when Thucydides portrays both as eager to justify a war with one another (1. 26-29).

A naval battle between Corcyra and Corinth ends when the Corinthians spot some Athenian ships that they mistake for the vanguard of a larger Athenian fleet. The arrival of these Athenian ships puts an end to a sea battle in which five Athenian ships, ostensibly sent only for Corcyra's defensive use, take offensive action against Corinth. This Athenian offensive violates the terms of the Thirty Years Peace of 445 BCE and is one of the two incidents that Thucydides identifies as the "openly expressed" causes of the Peloponnesian War (1. 23). This whole Corcyran affair depicts the attempt to compel with the threat of force as a strategy employed to provoke rather than prevent a war.

---

11 Reading *aitiai* with Ste. Croix as "openly expressed causes." Ste. Croix, G. E. M. 1972. *The Origins of the Peloponnesian War*. Ithaca: Cornell University Press, 53. Cf. Kagan, Donald. 1969. *The Outbreak of the Peloponnesian War*. Ithaca: Cornell University Press, 345; and Momigliano, A. D.. 1966. "Some Observations on Causes of War in Ancient Historiography." In *Studies in Historiography*. London: University of London Press, 112-26.

Thucydides reports another cause of the war that exhibits similar dynamics. This Potidaean episode unfolds in the aftermath of the Corinthian defeat at Corcyra, at a time when "Corinth was forming schemes for retaliation, and Athens suspected her hostility." (Strassler 1. 56). Athens' threat of force fails to compel its colony Potidaea, in north-eastern Greece, to comply and results in the Athenian troops marching a long distance to besiege the city (1. 61).

In the aftermath of these provocative episodes, Thucydides describes a surprising attempt at diplomacy by some Athenian representatives who were in Sparta "on other business" when the Spartan war council met to decide whether to keep the promise of some unnamed Spartan authorities to invade Attica if the Athenians attacked Potidaea.[12] These Athenians claim that Athens has a right to her empire and ask Sparta to delay its invasion. In response, the Spartan King, Archidamus, takes a moderate position and urges the Spartans to delay, but the Spartan assembly is emotionally aroused and votes "overwhelmingly" for war (Strassler 1. 73-79). Despite Athens' provocations, this vote establishes Sparta as the effective aggressor in the Peloponnesian War. From the Corinthians' speech at this council we learn that the role of aggressor is out of character for Sparta, which has a traditional honor code restricting it to defensive warfare (1. 68-71). In other passages, Thucydides tells us that the Spartans came to feel uncomfortable with this new-found aggressive role and attempt to reestablish this honor code later in the war (1. 118; 7. 18).[13]

---

12 See Kagan, *The Outbreak*, 293-4 for a discussion of why we should take their speech as a legitimate account of Athenian policy.

13 Zagorin, *Thucydides*, chapter 3; Kagan, *The Outbreak*, 299-316; Ste. Croix, *The Origins*, 56, 94.

The diplomatic language the Athenians use with the Spartans in 432 BCE takes the form of a justification and defense of Athenian imperialism.[14] This defense contrasts with the Athenians' denial of any obligation to justify their behavior in their dialogue with the Melians 16 years later, in 416 BCE. The Athenian envoys claim in this earlier justification that Athens has a "fair title" to the empire it built in the aftermath of the Persian Wars, during a time when the Greek states all feared another Persian invasion. The envoys cite this fear as Athens' principal motive for increasing its imperial power and list honor and self-interest as secondary motives. In their description, the Athenians express pride in their empire and their conviction that they hold their power justly. The Athenian language in the Melian Dialogue, by contrast, describes their empire as a burden and abandons all claims to be acting justly. What circumstances led to such a radical shift in the Athenians' perception of their own power?

From 432 to 416 BCE

At the Spartan war council in 432 BCE, the Corinthians describe the Athenians as motivated primarily by what Plato would call appetite. The Corinthians describe the Athenians as a people who "were born into the world to take no rest themselves and to give none to others" (Strassler, 1. 70). These acquisitive Athenians gauge success by actions rather than words. Thus, the Corinthians say of them: "a scheme unexecuted is with them a positive loss" (Strassler, 1. 70). This appetite manifests itself as the Athenians' perpetual and

14 See Orwin, Clifford. 1994. *The Humanity of Thucydides*. Princeton: Princeton University Press, 44-50.

irrational desire to have more, that "growing Athenian greatness" identified by Thucydides as the truest cause of the Peloponnesian War (Strassler 1. 23).

In Book Eight of the *Republic*, Plato links appetite to democracy. The democratic man and the democratic regime are ruled by appetite, the lowest part of the soul. Plato's democratic man knows no moderation, he "lives along day by day, gratifying the desire that occurs to him" (*Republic* 561c).[15]

The Corinthian description identifies the ways the Athenians display the democratic excesses of appetite. Plato's appetitive democrats seek pleasure and avoid pain. This classification accords with Thucydides' description of the Athenians' own behavior: they lose their appetite for war when they encounter the pain of the plague and regain it after a peace treaty is declared in 422 BCE. The Athenian vote in 415 BCE, during the peace treaty, to send an expedition to Sicily shows a resurgence of Athenian appetitive acquisitiveness, perhaps as a response to the unpleasant necessity of having continually to suppress revolts among their allies in the Aegean.

According to Plato, this democratic lifestyle prepares the way for tyranny (*Republic* 562C). "Too much freedom," Plato writes in Book Eight, "seems to change into nothing but too much slavery, both for private man and city" (*Republic* 564a). According to Thucydides, the Athenians were beginning as early as 431 BCE to feel enslaved to their empire. Thucydides records a speech that the Athenian statesman Pericles gave in that year as including an acknowledgement that the Athenian empire is in effect a tyranny. Addressing an Athenian assembly now eager for peace, Pericles admits that "what you hold is,

---

15 All translations of Plato's *Republic* are from Bloom, Allan. 1968. *The Republic of Plato*. New York: Harper Collins.

to speak somewhat plainly, a tyranny; to take it perhaps was wrong, but to let it go is unsafe" (Strassler, 2. 63). Although the Athenians may wish for a more moderate (and more pleasant) imperial policy, Pericles advises them to continue their aggression out of fear of the retaliation they would incur with any lessening of their power. In Pericles' assessment, the need to become more tyrannical is linked to the need to become more expedient. According to this doctrine of expedient self-interest, the Athenians must now overrule their inclinations and appetites in order to maintain their security.

At the same time, Pericles' comment acknowledges that this expedient interest may ultimately be against Athens' long-term security interest. Thucydides has already introduced this possibility, that Greece's hatred for Athens' harsh policies was a primary factor in the outbreak of war. "Men's feelings inclined much more to the Spartans," Thucydides writes about the outbreak of the war, "... so general was the indignation felt against Athens, whether by those who wished to escape from her empire, or were apprehensive of being absorbed in it" (Strassler, 2. 8; cf. 1, 22-4; 1. 139; 2. 72). Later in the *History*, both the Mytilenian Debate and the Melian Dialogue contain explicit arguments that Athens' interpretation of expedient self-interest increases the number of Athens' enemies and contributes to Athens' long-term security problems (3. 46; 5. 90; 5. 98).

Athens' increasingly expedient policies are accompanied by a shift in the Athenians' motivation for aggression. While the Corinthians described the Athenians as motivated before the war by appetite, Pericles describes them in the early years of the war as motivated primarily by fear. This shift is compatible with Plato's description of the movement from democracy to tyranny. While a democratic regime uses force to acquire the objects of its desire, a tyranny is enslaved to force. Plato's democracy, for example, is savage, but his tyranny is "the greatest and most savage slavery" (*Republic* 564a). The Corinthian description of the Athenians at the Spartan war council in 432 BCE focuses on the ways the Athenians use their power to get what they actively desire: "their designs are characterized by swiftness alike in conception and execution… they alone are enabled to call a thing hoped for a thing got, by the speed with which they act upon their resolutions" (Strassler, 1. 70). Pericles, on the other hand, focuses on the need to disregard the appetite's pursuit of pleasure and avoidance of pain and maintain a dispassionate policy of aggression. While the Corinthians emphasize the Athenian appetite for "the thing hoped for," Pericles emphasizes the need to exercise force even when it is unpleasant.

Athens' expedition to Melos in 416 BCE combines these motivations of appetite and fear in an interesting way. At the time of the Melian Dialogue, the Athenian Assembly's vote to send an expedition to Sicily is only six months away (6. 1). Although Thucydides does not make this point explicitly, the Athenians likely understand their aggression toward Melos in terms of their need to forestall revolts within their current empire while their navy is occupied attempting to expand it.

When the Athenian forces arrive at Melos in 416 BCE, the Athenians know their allies are so much driven by hatred that they would find cause for rebellion even in the existence of a strategic neutral such as Melos. The Athenians' fear of such rebellions is the primary motivation that the Athenian generals give in the Melian Dialogue for their aggression toward the neutral Melos: "it is islanders like yourselves, outside our empire... who would be the most likely to lead us into obvious danger" (Strassler, 5. 99). The danger comes not from Melos itself but from existing Athenian allies who are looking for any excuse to revolt. As a result, the Athenians have no positive appetite for this conquest and hope that they will be able to acquire Melos through threat alone, "without trouble" (Strassler, 5. 91). The Athenians characterize their aggression toward Melos as a necessary but onerous duty dictated to them by the terms of expedient self-interest.

Elsewhere in the *History*, Thucydides links Athens' interpretation of expediency to its need to use increasing levels of violence. In the Mytilenian Debate in Book Three, the Athenian demagogue Cleon makes the continual fear of revolt the explicit justification for Athens' increasingly violent strategies of deterrence. The Mytilenian Debate took place in 427 BCE, just months before the general Nicias' first, unsuccessful expedition to Melos. In his response to Cleon, the Athenian Diodotus raises the question of whether even the harshest punishment of Mytilene will be effective in deterring other Athenian allies from revolt.

Mytilene was the largest city on the island of Lesbos, itself the largest of the Ionian islands along the coast of Asia Minor. The Mytilenian revolt was organized by members of the city's aristocracy, who wished to turn the city and the island of Lesbos over to the Spartans. The Athenians used a show of force (100 ships against the Spartans' 40) in an unsuccessful attempt to deter the revolt. Once the revolt was underway and the Athenians were besieging the city, the commoners (the *demos*) of Mytilene betrayed the city to the Athenians.

The day before Thucydides' debate, the enraged Athenians had already voted to kill all the Mytilenian males, commoners and aristocrats alike. Cleon and Diodotus had been the strongest speakers in the debate leading up to that vote - Cleon in favor of killing all the Mytilenian males and Diodotus in favor of killing only the guilty aristocrats. Overnight, public feeling had shifted: "The morrow brought repentance with it and reflection on the horrid cruelty of a decree which condemned a whole city to the fate merited only by the guilty" (Strassler 3. 36). A reassembly convened and Cleon and Diodotus argue their positions a second time. In this second debate, Cleon argues that brutal violence is the only effective deterrent, Diodotus that the threat of death has never stopped rebellion. "Either some means of terror more terrible than death must be discovered," Diodotus says, "or it must be admitted that this restraint [of deterrence] is useless" (Strassler 3. 45). Interestingly, although Diodotus' position is now supported by the people's repentance and reflection, in the second vote, Cleon is still almost equally persuasive. Despite the strong public sentiment for overruling the previous day's death sentence, "the show of hands was almost equal" (Strassler 3. 49).

The closeness of this second vote shows that even when the Athenians find violent deterrence morally repugnant, they feel themselves strategically dependent on it. Although the second vote reinstated justice, the original vote and the closeness of the second vote illustrate how easily the policy of expedient realism can overcome moral sentiment. To put it in Plato's terms, the Athenians are growing increasingly tyrannized by their fear of their own allies.

The Athenians' preoccupation with their rebellious allies leads them to Melos, where they extend Cleon's preemptive policy to a neutral state and give Melos only two options: slavery or war. "All we can reasonably expect from this negotiation," the Melians lament at the outset of the Dialogue, "is war, if we prove to have right on our side and refuse to submit, or in the contrary case, slavery" (Strassler 5. 86). The Athenian force, we learn, consists of 38 ships, enough effectively to blockade the small island of Melos. In the next section, we will turn to the Melian Dialogue and consider why the Melians choose to resist.

The Melian Dialogue

Although the Athenian generals would like to speak to the people (the *demos*), the Melian aristocrats limit the meeting to a small group of aristocratic envoys. This is almost certainly because the Melian aristocrats fear that the commoners, ruled by a simple calculation of self-interest, would vote to surrender.

In response to the Melians' insistence that the meeting be private, the Athenians propose "a method more cautious still" and suggest that the two sides dispense with set speeches (Strassler 5. 86). They ask the Melian aristocrats to dispense with an oratorical style because "noble phrases" would here make for a "lengthy and unconvincing speech" (Lattimore, 5. 89). Commentators have struggled with the question of whether the dialogue style grants advantage to the Melians or the Athenians.[16] In order to under-

---

16 See Morrison, James. 2006. *Reading Thucydides*. Columbus: The Ohio State University Press, 81-83 for an overview of the scholarship.

stand who gets the advantage here, we need to find out what kind of a dialogue this is.

The Athenians offer the Melians the dialogue format to allow the Melians to "respond immediately to whatever is said that sounds unfavorable" (Lattimore 5. 85). In response, the Melians observe "that you have come as the judges in your own cause" and conclude from the presence of the fleet that the Athenians are not going to be interested in their responses (Strassler, 5. 86).

The Melians point out that the give-and-take format of the dialogue is meaningless unless both sides are open to persuasion. According to Plato, the willingness to consider the interlocutors' arguments is a crucial principle of dialogue. The opening of Plato's *Republic* illustrates the problem that Plato sees with combining force and dialogue. In Plato's text, even before the conversation gets underway the possibility of dialogue is called into question by Polemarchus' threat to force Socrates to come to his home and participate. Let us look at that interaction between Polemarchus and Socrates:

> 'Well,' Polemarchus said, 'do you see how many of us there are?' 'Of course'. 'Well, then,' he said, 'either prove stronger than these men or stay here.' 'Isn't there still one other possibility…' I said,, 'our persuading you that you must let us go?' 'Could you really persuade,' he said, 'if we don't listen?' 'There's no way,' said Glaucon (*Republic* 327C).

Polemarchus' final question (Could you really persuade if we don't listen?) and Glaucon's response (There's no way) illustrate why Plato finds force and dialogue incompatible. If the agent threatens to use force, he is not open to the persuasion of argument. Although the Melian aristocrats agree to the dialogue format, they point out that the presence of the Athenian fleet is incompatible with the aims of dialogue: "The fairness of instructing one another peacefully cannot be faulted, but a readiness for war right now instead of eventually is obviously inconsistent" (Lattimore 5. 86). Because the Athenians have come to it armed for war, the Melian Dialogue is not dialogic in any philosophical sense. Rather, it is closer to what the Greeks called *eristic*, a style of argument that seeks victory rather than understanding.[17]

The Athenians' attitude toward the Melians is similar to Thrasymachus' attitude toward Socrates in Book One of Plato's *Republic*. Thrasymachus' behavior illustrates how the dialogue format can be violently co-opted by a speaker who has no interest in the opinions of his interlocutor but is rather seeking victory in argument. The substance of Thrasymachus' argument is that the only operative justice is the advantage of the stronger. The Athenians' reasoning is similar: "Justice," they tell the Melians, "is only in question between equals in power, while the strong do what they can and the weak suffer what they must" (Strassler, 5. 89). In the *Republic*, Socrates attempts to persuade Thrasymachus that justice and violence are incompatible.

Thrasymachus is not persuaded; he identifies his superior strength as the justice of his position and attacks Socrates at the moment that Socrates draws the opposing conclusion that "it is not the work of the just man to harm either a friend or anyone else but of his opposite, the unjust man" (*Republic* 335d). Plato describes

17 See Kerferd, G. B.. 1981. *The Sophistic Movement*. Cambridge: Cambridge University Press, 62.

this attack as having a physical component: "when we paused and I said this, he could no longer keep quiet; hunched up like a wild beast, he flung himself at us as if to tear us to pieces" (*Republic* 336d). Thrasymachus uses his strength to legitimate his position in the dialogue. If he cannot conquer in argument, he will resort to violence. "You won't be able to overpower me in the argument," he declares to Socrates. Socrates, on the other hand, sees dialogue as an activity of reason that requires both parties to be open to legitimate persuasion.

Like the Melians, Socrates is not equal to his opponent in strength. Fortunately, Socrates has allies. In Plato's *Republic*, Socrates' other interlocutors maintain his standards for dialogue and do not tolerate Thrasymachus' violence: "When Thrasymachus had said this, he had it in mind to go away... but those present didn't let him and forced him to stay put and present an argument for what had been said" (*Republic* 344d).

In Thucydides' dialogue, the Melians are similar to the frightened but persistent Socrates. Unlike Socrates, however, they have no allies present to force their belligerent opponents to cooperate. The Spartans have not come to their aid, although the Melians still hope they will, not for reasons of expediency but for the sake of honor. The Melians believe that honor is a significant political motive and hope that "what we want in power will be made up by the alliance of the Spartans, who are bound, if only for very shame, to come to the aid of their kindred" (Strassler, 5. 104). The Melians, unlike the Athenians, still have some trust in the bonds of friendship between independent states. Although they recognize that friendship is not an expedient motive, they hope that their friends will feel honor-bound to defend them against unjust Athenian aggression.

The Athenians are quick to mock the Melians for valuing friendship and honor: "in your beliefs about the Spartans, which lead to your faith that they will help you out of honor, we find a touching naiveté yet do not envy your folly" (Strassler, 5. 105). Spartan honor, according to the Athenians, is only a hypocritical name for Spartan self-interest:

> The Spartans, when their own interests or their country's laws are in question, are the worthiest men alive; of their conduct toward others much might be said, but no clearer idea of it could be given than by shortly saying that of all the men we know they are most conspicuous in considering what is agreeable honorable, and what is expedient just (Strassler, 5. 105).

The Athenians accuse the Spartans of engaging in the hypocrisy of cloaking their own expedient self-interest in the nominal language of justice and honor, and see their own rejection of diplomacy and justice as a more honest acknowledgement that the strong care only for their own self-interest. "We shall not trouble you," they tell the Melians, "with specious pretenses either of how we have a right to our empire because we overthrew the Mede, or are now attacking you because of wrong that you have done us" (Strassler, 5. 89). In keeping with their new realist and morally relativist rhetoric, the Athenians dismiss this honor as an empty term: "the name of disgrace, by the power of the word's fascination, induces men still able to foresee what is in store for them to fall knowingly into irremediable disasters, their actions overcome by a phrase" (Lattimore, 5. III).

This rejection of justice and honor is a new development for the Athenians. Before the outbreak of the war, Thucydides portrays the Athenians attempting to justify to Sparta on moral grounds their right to their empire. In the early years of the war, Thucydides portrays the Athenian statesman Pericles acknowledging that Athens may have used unjust means to acquire its empire. In Pericles' speech, justice had a real meaning, even though he claimed that state security needed to override it. Similarly, the obligation of justice was operative even in Cleon's speech urging for the killing of all the Mytilenian males. In that speech, Cleon argued that not just the aristocratic perpetrators but all the Mytilenians were guilty of engaging in "deliberate and wanton aggression" and that the violent retaliation would be punishment "as their crime requires" (Strassler, 3. 39). Diodotus' counterargument also includes a reckoning of justice as a real Athenian motive, although he chooses to argue rather that a strategy of leniency would be expedient.

In writing of the early years of the war, Thucydides calls attention to the way values such as justice, courage, and moderation break down during wartime. In a rare passage of authorial commentary on the description of the revolt of Corcyra in 427 BCE, Thucydides describes how morals erode during revolution. Here Thucydides demonstrates the shift by contrasting the new meanings with the traditional values they pervert:

> Words had to change their ordinary meanings and to take that which was now given them. Reckless audacity came to be considered the courage of a loyal supporter; prudent hesi-

tation, specious cowardice; moderation was held to be a cloak for unmanliness; ability to see all sides of a question incapacity to act on any (Strassler, 3. 82).

These examples are all from the first few years of the war and illustrate how the circumstances of war corrode an acknowledged moral tradition. As the war progresses, the Athenians find it increasingly difficult to reconcile expediency and justice. Diodotus states this difficulty explicitly when he tells the Athenians that, "as for Cleon's idea that in punishment the claims of justice and expediency can both be satisfied, facts do not confirm the possibility of such a combination" (Strassler, 3. 47). At Melos, the Athenian generals reject this moral dilemma by denying that justice has any meaning beyond the right of the stronger; they admit at the outset that only specious pretense could construe their behavior as just. The Athenians no longer see the need to extend justice to those who are weaker than they, for they are now convinced that "the strong do what they can and the weak suffer what they must" (Strassler, 5. 89).

From a political and intellectual point of view, this idea reflects the radical free thinking and utilitarianism introduced into Athenian discourse during the early years of the war by the sophists at the invitation of Pericles. The new ideas of so-called sophists such as Gorgias and others under Pericles's patronage contributed to a rich intellectual culture in Athens during the early war years.[18] Gorgias, for example, made his first visit to Athens in 427 BCE, a few months before the Athenians' first, unsuccessful expedition to Melos. Sophists such as Gorgias dismissed traditional morality in favor of moral relativism, and introduced realism and expediency as

---

18   Zagorin, *Thucydides*, 20-22; Kerferd, *The Sophistic Movement*, 15-23.

the terms of political discourse. In 416 BCE, the Athenian generals at Melos take up these ideas and use them to form a justification for their strategy of unprovoked aggression.

The Peloponnesian War created countless occasions where the verbal critique of traditional morality offered by the sophistic movement expanded into the realm of real force and violence. The sophists promoted ideas that admittedly "had a corrosive effect upon inherited beliefs and moral principles."[19] The Melian Dialogue exhibits the sophistic techniques of eristic and antilogy, so much so that Thucydides likely intends it to model the latest fashion in sophistry.[20] Unlike political sophistry, however, the outcome of the Melian Dialogue will be for the Melians a matter of life or death, and the Athenians' eristic is far more than a rhetorical display since their navy has come prepared to use force if the Melians do not submit in the argument.

Although the Athenians have dismissed honor as an empty phrase, the Melians' choice not to submit to the Athenians' threat is made for reasons of honor. The Melian aristocrats are spirited, their pride and honor are more important to them than death. Violent deterrence will not work with them for the reasons Diodotus pointed out in the Mytilenian Debate: they are people who do not act consistently out of expedient self-interest. Just as Diodotus predicted, the Melian resistance is not based on any calculation of expediency but on their hope that their own just cause will prevail. The Athenian arguments about expediency only strengthen the Melians' resolve to resist as a point of honor. "Surely then," the Melians conclude, "if you take such desperate action to keep from

19 Zagorin, *Thucydides*, 21.
20 Ibid, 21, 106.

losing your empire, and those already in thrall do to be delivered, it is complete baseness and cowardice for us, still free, not to go to every length before being enslaved" (Lattimore, 5. 100).

We learn from Herodotus' *History* that only 65 years before, the Persian threat of force similarly strengthened the Athenians themselves in their resolve to resist as a point of honor. In 480 BCE the Persian general Mardonius used the threat of overwhelming force to attempt to compel the Athenians to surrender. Herodotus records the Athenian response to Mardonius as almost identical to the Melians' current response to them:

> We know of ourselves that the power of [Persia] is many times greater than our own; therefore, you need not throw that in our face. Yet we have such a hunger for freedom that we will fight as long as we are able (Grene, 8. 140-4).

In the Melian Dialogue, the Athenians seem proud that their new language of realism is free from the insincerity of the strained rhetoric that attempted to conjoin expediency and justice. In this new Machiavellian language, the motive of honor is an illusion employed by the naïve and helpless. The outright rejection of honor and justice as legitimate political motives is clearly a recent development for the Athenians. This comparison of Thucydides' Melian Dialogue with Herodotus' report of the Athenians' own earlier resistance exposes the irony implicit in the Athenian argument that a weaker state should surrender to them based on calculations of expediency.

In addition to being ironic, the Athenian insistence on the narrow terms of expediency also serves as literary foreshadowing of the fate of the Athenians in Sicily, in which any merited mercy is denied by the savage retaliation of the Syracusans. The Melian aristocrats urge the Athenians to adopt a more strategic, broader definition of expediency. "On your own downfall," they tell the Athenians, "you would set the example for the heaviest retribution" (Lattimore, 5. 90).

Nonetheless the Athenians will not listen to any arguments of contingency and they preemptively restrict the Melians to the narrow terms of expedient self-interest: "If you have met to reason about presentiments of the future, or for anything else than to consult for the safety of your state upon the facts that you see before you, we will cease talking; otherwise we will go on" (Lattimore, 5. 87).

Despite the Athenians' threat to end the dialogue if this topic is brought up again, the Melians later return to the theme of Athenian security. To the Athenians' admission of their concern that "our subjects would suppose… that we do not attack [you] because of fear," the Melians respond that the Athenians are using an ineffective strategy if their objective is to make their empire more secure:

> But do you consider that there is no security in the policy which we indicate? How can you avoid making enemies of all existing neutrals who shall look at our case and conclude from it that one day or another you will attack them? And what is this but to make greater the enemies that you have already, and to force others to become so who would otherwise have never thought of it? (Strassler, 5. 98).

The Athenians dismiss this argument for the practical reason that they now fear their own allies far more than the enmity of any remaining independent states.

The Melian expedition is a component of an ineffective Athenian strategy of controlling its empire with violent deterrence, and the Melian Dialogue illustrates the way the threat of violence provokes spirited resistance. Here again, Plato's *Republic* can supply us with terminology that maps readily onto Thucydides' account of the progression of the Melian Dialogue.[21] Plato's Socrates describes how suffering injustice triggers the spirit to fight to the death:

> What about when a man believes he's being done injustice? Doesn't his spirit in this case boil and become harsh and form an alliance for battle with what seems just; and, even if it suffers in hunger, cold and everything of the sort, doesn't it stand firm and conquer, and not cease from its noble efforts before it has succeeded, or death intervenes? (*Republic* 440c)

Socrates' argument that men who have suffered injustice will fight describes the Melians, who end the dialogue resolved to "go to every length before being enslaved."

The Melians respond like the spirited man Socrates describes in the *Republic* who believes he is being done an injustice – they accept the risks associated with justice and nobility despite the Athenians' attempt to devalue all such ideals. Honor is more than just a phrase to the Melian aristocrats and their decision to resist meets the requirements of *jus ad bellum* in that it is justified resistance to unprovoked aggression.

---

21 Cf. Lebow, "Thucydides and Deterrence," 179.

Lessons from the Melian Dialogue

The Melian Dialogue is not a dialogue in any Platonic sense. If we were to find a term for it, it should more appropriately be called the Melian Eristic. Yet even eristic, with its techniques for seeking victory in argument, is only rhetoric. The presence of an Athenian fleet prepared to use force makes it impossible to find in this so-called dialogue any exchange of ideas. The unquestionable credibility of the Athenian threat of force inspires the Melian aristocrats to impassioned resistance in the name of justice, honor, and freedom. The outcome is far from being without the "trouble" that the Athenians claimed at the outset they wished to avoid. The Athenians conduct a six months siege until an act of treachery by the Melian *demos* gives them access to the city. When the Athenians had taken the city, Thucydides reports, they "put to death all the grown men whom they took, and sold the women and children for slaves, and subsequently sent out five hundred colonists and settled the place themselves" (Strassler, 5. 116).

By the terms of Plato's *Republic*, the injustice of the Athenian assault on Melos is a symptom of a tyrannical regime that has redefined its moral terminology to support a fear-based strategy requiring the continual escalation of violence. This Athenian strategy is dictated by a narrow definition of expediency that excludes justice and honor as practical political motives. Intellectually, this breakdown of traditional morality created the conditions for Socrates' radical attempts to find philosophical definitions of justice and honor and Plato's subsequent attempt to focus political philosophy on the problem of finding a universal principle of justice. Politically and economically, the injustices perpetrated in the name of this tyrannical realism were costly for Athens, which had to spend a large part of its resources and its energy controlling its own imperial allies.

My intention here has been to illustrate a process that has psychological, historical, and moral dimensions. While Plato describes the chain reaction between fear and violence as a function of human psychology, Thucydides describes it as a historical truth. The relationship between fear, threats and violence is a fundamental feature of Thucydides' thought and constitutes for him the basis of the "truest cause" of the Peloponnesian War: "For I consider the truest cause the one least openly expressed, that increasing Athenian greatness and the resulting fear among the Lacedaemonians made going to war inevitable" (Lattimore, 1. 23). Thucydides' perception of the inevitability with which fear leads to violence frames his entire history.

If we borrow some terminology from Plato, who wrote only a few decades after the events at Melos, we have a fairly complete picture of a process that we all recognize as still operative in our own times. In his seeking "to articulate an understanding of human affairs that transcends that fostered by any regime,"[22] Thucydides offers a framework from which we can view our conflicts, past and present, with greater understanding and cautionary insight.

---

22 Orwin, *The Humanity of Thucydides*, 11.

Chapter 6

Aristotle: A Moralist for Our Times

Only six months after their so-called dialogue with the Melians, the Athenians voted to send an expensive naval campaign to Sicily, in the hopes of expanding their empire toward the west. In Thucydides' account of the deliberations within the Athenian assembly, the Athenian demagogues in favor of the expedition make one specious argument after another for why Athens' calculated self-interest entailed this costly and ambitious offensive, at a time when Athens' existing subject states were openly rebellious. Thucydides' history closes with the misfortunes and eventual defeat of this campaign. Soon after, the battered, bankrupt Athens lost the Peloponnesian War, and with it, its political autonomy. Thucydides' unmistakable final message is that Athenian hubris led to Athenian downfall. He uses a special word for the particular brand of arrogance that, unchecked in their political assembly, destroyed the Athenians: *pleonexia*, translated as 'greed', but literally 'the inclination toward more.'

Into this moral vacuum emerge philosophers such as Aristotle (384-322 BCE) who were prepared to rethink what it means to be a human being. In Aristotle we find the fullest expression of Greek humanism. In his *Nichomachean Ethics* particularly, but also in other writings, Aristotle explores what it means to be human, engaging in complex and modulated interactions both with other human beings and with the world we find ourselves in. It is this humanist tradition that I call strategic humanism, because it guides us to effective, moral engagement with the situations we face, and equips us to respond to circumstances that we cannot predict in advance. Aristotle's ethics are an ethics for the real world. For Aristotle, effective moral action is not dogmatic. As something essentially interactive, moral action cannot be worked out in advance, prior to our immersion in whatever situation calls for our response.

It is a fascinating historical phenomenon that secular moral philosophy was born in Athens, long the cultural center of Greece, at a time of catastrophic moral failure. One key factor in the nexus of conditions that led to its birth was that the Greek gods did not leave their people with any moral teachings given by revelation, i.e. in the form of Scripture. The Greek people would have to work out morality for themselves, independently of any guidance from the divine. Add to that the Athenians' devastating military defeat, and the conditions were ripe for a systematic and considered reflection on human morality.

The written tradition begins with Plato (424 -328 BCE), whose dialogues depict a character Socrates, who explored the problem of why human beings lack knowledge about moral concepts such as virtue or justice. Socrates pointed out that if we had *knowledge* of virtue, we would always act on it, just as when we have *knowledge* of how to solve a geometry problem, we proceed to solve it without mistake. Plato's dialogues highlight the philosophical imperative to search for the essence of virtue through reasoning and dialectic. As a result, Plato rejected the passions and the appetites as ineffective and unreliable guides to right action. Plato was convinced that the concepts of virtue must have perfect, rational definitions, even if the knowledge of these eludes us as human beings. This led Plato to his Theory of Forms, in which he posits the existence of some supranatural domain in which all of these pure concepts of virtue exist. While philosophically profound, Plato's work can have troubling aspects, for his idealism is intimidating to a student looking for moral guidance in the midst of a hectic, active life. In addition, the practical consequences of Plato's idealism remain unclear, and a literal reading of a text like the *Republic* illustrates the problem of trying to approach real life problems with the intellect alone. The statesman and scholar Christopher Hill sums up the dangers of a strictly rationalist approach to the problems of political life:

> Socrates, in Plato's *Republic*, intellectually attempts to design a polis. The result is repulsive, perhaps an ironic demonstration of how pure intellect in its search for political utopia can produce a tyranny that would drain humanity of its capacity for virtue.[1]

To be fair, it is not clear that the city designed in speech in the *Republic* is intended to be taken literally. Perhaps it is a thought-experiment to illustrate the extent to which injustice is embedded in human nature. However, Plato's lofty philosophical exercises do not help a student who would like to take away from her reading some practical moral guidelines to better her way of life in the active world.

Aristotle himself criticizes Plato's idealism early in the *Nichomachean Ethics*, pointing out that while Plato was "a friend," Aristotle himself believes that the search for truth about moral matters

---

1   Hill, *Grand Strategies*, 28.

demands a much more pragmatic approach than the ideal rationalism of the Theory of Forms (NE 1096a13-14).[2] Raphael's famous
painting, "The School of Athens," illustrates the contrast between
these two approaches. In the painting, Plato points upward toward
the pure realm of the Form of the Good, a realm unattainable by
mortal humans. Aristotle gestures toward the ground, in accord
with his conviction that it is in this world that we need to act out
our moral worth.

Indeed, Aristotle took a very different approach to moral philosophy than did his teacher Plato. Aristotle's interest was in finding a
more realistic framework within which an active person, whether
a politician, an entrepreneur, a military figure, or other, can find a
guide to ethical life choices. Aristotle's response was aligned with
the Greek humanist tradition we have traced here, a tradition in
which the individual can make a complex assessment of a situation,
and respond to it on the spot. However, the individuals we have
traced so far in these studies have used their intellectual, intuitive,
and creative talents without a stable, internal framework for reflection on the moral content of their actions and their consequences.
Aristotle introduces the terms of morality, in order to give virtue a
place alongside material efficacy as a necessary criterion for effective action.

Moderation is the centerpiece of Aristotle's moral theory. Rather
than focus on the elusive concept of virtue, Aristotle begins with the
assumption that in real life, moral deficiency and excess are readily
apparent within a community, so that a practical moral framework

---

2   All translations from the *Nicomachean Ethics* (NE) are from Aristotle. 1999.
    Nicomachean Ethics. Translated by Terence Irwin. Indianapolis: Hackett
    Publishing Company.

is already available to guide the would-be moral agent toward the moderate middle where virtue is found. Rather than studying virtue as an abstract principle, Aristotle links it to the particulars of the situation: the personality and inclination of the agent, the circumstances, the other people involved, the timing, and other variables. If the action is moderate, that is, if it is done for the right reasons, in the right ways, at the right time, using the right means, then its agent deserves the label of virtue (NE 1106b21-23).

The Aristotelian understanding of virtue combines its external aspect, which is the action itself, with its internal aspect, the way the agent generates the behavior within herself. In this Aristotelian model, the action is matched to its agent by a complex matrix of conditions internal to the agent, that include her knowledge of what she is doing, her decision to take this action for its own sake and not for other self-interested motives, and her ability to generate such actions consistently. Aristotle says this about the inadequacy of the external action alone, and the need for it to be aligned with these internal qualities in the agent:

> For actions in accord with the virtues to be done temperately or justly it does not suffice that they themselves have the right qualities. Rather, the agent must also be in the right state when he does them. First, he must know that he is doing virtuous actions; second, he must decide on them, and decide on them for themselves; and third, he must also do them from a firm and unchanging state. (NE 1105a29-34)

Because of his interest in the internal state of the human being, Aristotle's sense of how virtue manifests itself is quite different from its depiction in the warrior communities depicted in earlier chapters. In the Homeric community, right and wrong were defined by the self-interest of the group, and are only found in interaction, with no internal standard to determine moral action as such. Ajax accuses Achilles of betrayal for staying out of the fight when his comrades needed him, but neither he nor the others at the embassy in Book Nine frames the question of Achilles' withdrawal from the fight in universal moral terms. The Homeric dialect lacks words that denote the requisites for a coherent framework of an internal morality, words like "virtue" and "character." Similarly, the characters in Herodotus' *History* lack a framework within which to reflect internally on the morality of their own actions. Thucydides, who himself seems keenly aware that moral concepts have real meaning, depicts Greece as falling ever more deeply into moral relativism as the Peloponnesian War goes on.

It is Aristotle who introduces us to a moral humanism, in which humans are understood as beings whose morality has both an internal and external component, beings who display their commitment to good character through enacting behaviors directed toward both self and other that are consistent with rational principles. Rather than trying to separate ourselves in some Cartesian fashion from our environment in order to isolate our reasoning about morality, we find here an integrated way of being moral, one that acknowledges our pre-existing ethical obligations to community and world, yet maintains that good character is an enduring possession that an individual can acquire through some rationally directed process. Aristotle's work represents the culmination of the Greek humanist spirit we have traced from Homer through Thucydides, in that it respects political and military activity, and the human spirit and ambition that drives it, and yet extends the notion of moral quality to the individual's internal world in a coherent and accessible way.

Aristotle finds a unique solution to the problem of providing morality with an internal as well as external component. He posits a principle, the *orthos logos*, "correct reason," that provides the would-be moral agent with a rational way to choose among various real-world options. Yet the principle is not prescriptive, it is descriptive, designed to help the agent recognize a pattern of good judgment that applies to all the components of moral deliberation: the choice of outcomes, the choice of means to get to that outcome, how to time and implement these means, and how to conduct oneself emotionally toward all these variables. Aristotle places an emphasis on child development, realizing that the habits one learns in childhood will retain their influence over what kinds of behaviors one takes pleasure in as an adult. Hence Aristotle advises us to look at the kinds of things we take pleasure or pain in, and to become aware that good character requires that these things align with moral behavior. Here again, we see how the external action has to align with an internal state in the agent's character. "Virtues," Aristotle says, "are concerned with actions and feelings" (NE 1104b14).

In order to establish Aristotle's humanist approach to the problem of morality, it is helpful to contrast his humanism with that displayed by another great moral philosopher, separated from him by around 2000 years, the German Idealist Immanuel Kant (1724-1804). Kant's investigation of morality owes much to the mind-body split, and the possibility of isolating pure reason, theories that were introduced by Bacon and Descartes. In his famous *Critique of*

Pure Reason, Kant searches for the elements of pure reason, those elements of reason that, untouched by experience, would ensure reason's objectivity and give it a domain of its own within which to operate. In his moral theory, presented in the *Groundwork for the Metaphysics of Morals* and *The Metaphysics of Morals*, and further elaborated in the *Critique of Practical Reason*, Kant expands this project into a search for a universal moral principle that would serve as a positive answer to the question about virtue's essence. Kant labelled this principle the categorical imperative, in order to illustrate its character as a universally binding moral law. Kant's absolutism located morality in the agent's performance of an act of pure reason, and refused to consider the contingent circumstances that characterize the act itself as contributors to the moral content of a behavior. Kant's moral philosophy is a testament to the growing influence during the Enlightenment of the Cartesian assumption that mind could find its way independently of the body.

The Kantian idea that moral action consists in adherence to a fixed inner rule has influenced the way the modern reader interprets Aristotle's writings. As philosopher Nancy Sherman observes, "the Kantian influence has inevitably shaped the translation and meaning of key words. In particular, it has shaped the meaning of *orthos logos*, literally correct or right reason (or reasoning), but under a Kantian gloss rendered 'right rule', 'rational principle'."[3] The Kantian predisposition is for a static rule for virtue, much like an arithmetic ruler, that can be held up against a particular case to yield a quantitative determination. Within Aristotle's integrated moral theory, the notion of such a 'one size fits all' rule is antithet-

---

3   Sherman, Nancy. 1989. *The Fabric of Character: Aristotle's Theory of Virtue.* Oxford: Clarendon Press, 23.

ical to the nature of the subject under investigation, for morality, he claims, is not an exact science, but rather one in which "our premises are things that hold good usually (but not universally)" (NE 1094B20-23). Moral conduct should not impose an artificially universal stamp on particulars that don't conform. As Aristotle says, "Our present discussion does not aim… at study; for the purpose of our examination is not to know what virtue is, but to become good" (NE 1103B2-29).

Aristotle's notion of the good goes beyond an understanding of the concept, and it includes some sense that this morally acting individual should and hopefully will thrive in the world. This notion of thriving draws on Aristotle's word for happiness, *eudaemonia*, which translates as "blessedness," or "experiencing good fortune," and which Aristotle explicitly links to moral behavior. This robust definition of happiness as reflective of a pattern of moral choices in an active life means that virtue will look different in different individuals. Hence, Aristotle concludes that the premises of his inquiry cannot be taken as universals, and advises us to "be satisfied to draw conclusions of the same sort" of ambiguity as the subject matter warrants (NE 1094b23). The very study of morality requires an integrated approach, one that considers the way moral decisions must be made amidst changing circumstances by active men and women who may not have much leisure to consider their choice.

By investing virtue with this combination of external and internal factors, Aristotle establishes morality as an active principle that combines all the qualities of human response: reason, emotion, and the resultant action. In his *Nicomachean Ethics*, Aristotle considers the question of virtue alongside an inquiry into the particulars of how it arises in the normal course of human development. The responsibility of each individual is to assess and respond to situations in such a way that she can bring her thoughts, feelings, and actions into a unified whole that displays the "kinship with virtue" she has developed by her conscious dedication to acting rightly (NE 1179b20-31). In practical terms, this organizing of inner and outer may have to happen quickly; there is no guarantee that one will have leisure for a protracted deliberation. A moral posture within one's environment requires that one continually attends to one's character, and thus stands ready to act at any time. Far from the Cartesian model, in which the mind can retreat from the physical world, Aristotle understands the human being as essentially and always in interaction with the environment.

To be compatible with morality, this interaction cannot be accidental, something that one does out of mindless habit, or with some ulterior end in mind. The moral actor must choose virtue, in order to "activate" the moral framework within which the choice makes sense. Aristotle defines the human good as "activity of the soul in accord with virtue," and goes on to establish a kind of feedback loop, in which the more one engages in this activity, the more one will shape oneself into the kind of person who consistently reflects the virtues, both internally and externally (NE 1098a17-18). This model grants a kind of truth to the idea that justice is what just people do. Aristotle avoids circularity here, because of the expectation that each agent is in ongoing interaction with the world, and that it is in this activity that the virtues are either present or not.

If the Aristotelian *orthos logos* is not intended to be interpreted in Kantian fashion as a neutral, universal rule, what is its role in ensuring moral conduct? Aristotle offers it as a framework that accounts for how a certain kind of person will respond to the choices and demands of her environment. According to Sherman, the *orthos logos* is not intended as a neutral rule, but "remains much closer to the particulars" than the Kantian moral imperative. Confronted with the need to act, the *orthos logos* offers "a way of 'improvising' and 'conjecturing' given experience and what is now at hand."[4] This does not mean improvising in the sense of something one makes up, but in the sense that musicians understand jazz as music that must arise spontaneously, yet be subject to strict requirements of form and technique. In this case, the acquisition of technique is what sets good character apart from the weak character. According to this view, virtue cannot be codified; it is exhibited by the individual of good character as a sequence of finely tuned responses to the moral demands of one's environment. The philosopher John McDowell puts it this way:

> Occasion by occasion, one knows what to do, if one does, not by applying universal principles but by being a certain kind of person: one who sees situations in a certain, distinctive way.[5]

Aristotle's guideline, the *orthos logos*, asks the would-be moral agent to calibrate her thoughts, feelings, and actions to the situation, so that she thinks, feels, and acts "for the right things, in the right ways, at the right times."[6] This is Aristotle's doctrine of

---

4 Sherman, *The Fabric of Character*, 25

5 McDowell, John. 1979. "Virtue and Reason." In *Aristotle's Ethics: Critical Essays*. Edited by Nancy Sherman. Lanham: Rowman and Littlefield Press, 121-144.

6 This formula is repeated again and again throughout the *Nicomachean Ethics*. See, for example, 1119b16-19.

virtue as a mean, and the touchstone of this guideline is that the moral response must properly be connected to the environment, that is, calibrated and attuned to whatever external conditions one encounters. Such a response cannot be calculated ahead of time. The deliberation that leads to the individual's chosen action can only be undertaken once the particular contingencies are known. The fluidity of this model of virtue ethics makes it highly adaptable to the ethical questions that arise in our fast-paced contemporary technological environment.

Aristotle's formulation can be compared to Clausewitz's understanding of how a great general operates in war, using a kind of intuition, a *coup d'oiel*, to size up a situation whose variables cannot be assessed scientifically. Clausewitz himself places this type of judgment in a moral context:

> The moral reaction, the ever-changeful form of things, makes it necessary for the chief actor to carry in himself the whole mental apparatus of his knowledge, that anywhere and at every pulse-beat he may be capable of giving the requisite decision from himself.[7]

There are many advocates for a neo-Aristotelian approach to the complex issues that emerge in today's highly technologized world. To give some examples for context, consider that one ethicist writing in the context of the contemporary debate about the ethics of space exploration says, "The properties of the moral agent, not the properties of his/her environment are the key to doing the right thing, and no matter how strange the circumstances an explorer may

---

7   Clausewitz, *On War*, II, II, 46.

find herself in, she always has access to knowledge about her own state of mind."[8] This writer advocates for the Aristotelian model, in which the agent carries her moral responsiveness with her wherever she goes, as a property of self.

Such an approach avoids many of the pitfalls of utilitarian, or consequentialist ethics, also a post-Cartesian development, which in its effort to statistically assess the cost-benefit calculus of a situation can narrow the terms of value to the point that decision-making overlooks complex realities of culture and society. As another example, a contemporary anthropological study concludes that an Aristotelian model would be more effective than a data-focused scientific model at evaluating quality of life among indigenous peoples because:

> Value is featured by diversity and different human interpretations of wellbeing or happiness, and the net value gains in CBA (cost-benefit analysis) do not necessarily produce certain amounts or types of happiness as desired by society. This is attributed to the fact that the money-value steered worldview of CBA is unable to account for a large portion of the "net worth" attached to non-market components which contribute substantially to wellbeing improvement or happiness.[9]

This author also understands that the Aristotelian notion of thriving cannot be reduced to a statistical reckoning based on access to the external resource of money.

---

8   Reiman, Saara. 2009. "Is Space an Environment?" In *Space Policy* issue 25. Cambridge, MA: Elsevier, 86.

9   Choy, Yee Keong. 2018. "Cost-benefit Analysis, Values, Wellbeing and Ethics: An Indigenous Worldview Analysis." In *Ecological Economics* issue 145. Cambridge, MA: Elsevier, 8.

This insistence on the agent's ability to assess complex situations means that, for Aristotle, virtue is not something natural or inborn, but rather a way of organizing the complex moral phenomena of one's environment, a way that begins in childhood with the instilment of good habits, continues with education, and extends into adulthood as a conscious and ongoing effort to exercise one's moral quality through one's actions in the world.[10]

The social sciences have demonstrated the importance of the earliest years of a child's life to his or her ethical development. Structure and regularity in the home environment have been scientifically linked to a child's chances for a good life, as are the involvement of attentive caregivers who are able to set clear boundaries. This work validates Aristotle's humanist understanding of the importance of habituation. The importance of these early years to a child's sense of ethical obligation is especially apparent when a child's social environment has been too strict or too permissive. As Aristotle says, the states conducive to virtue "tend to be ruined by excess and deficiency" (NE 1104a13). A child fortunate enough to have the influence of good rule-setters still needs to be obedient: "If the child is not obedient and subordinate to its rulers, it will go far astray" (NE 1119b3).

As the child grows older, habituation continues to supply moral modes of conduct in the form of social or familial norms that should be observed even if an understanding of *why* this behavior is good is not present. Consider the exasperated parent who says to the querulous child, "Do it because I said so!" A young person might exhibit the communal virtues out of a desire to please, or a fear of

---

10 Cf. NE 1114b1-13.

being ostracized if she does not. Children and adolescents may do the right thing out of fear of punishment or conformity to the norm long before their judgment is mature enough to make reliable moral decisions across a variety of circumstances. Ultimately, though, Aristotle insists that the transition be made from habit to mature moral identity, and that the moral agent must choose the virtuous action knowingly, and choose it for its own sake (NE 1105a30-35).

Actions are not the only component of morality that can be influenced by habituation. For an action to be moral in Aristotle's view, the emotional response must be appropriate to what is chosen, and this is not a matter of chance. Appropriate emotional responses and empathy must be cultivated and developed, through role modeling and suggestion. In this view, children learn what emotions are appropriate to what circumstances through being told, and through watching adults display emotional responses that are moderated by reason, that is, emotional responses that are neither excessive nor deficient. Young people learn by experience to recognize the moral successes and failures displayed by those around them. Through witnessing just as well as unjust acts, friendship as well as enmity, young people learn to locate the space in which good judgments are made. This is the space that Aristotle calls "the mean," flanked by the extremes. Aristotle uses the examples of courage and generosity to illustrate the mean. Too much courage is foolhardiness, too little is cowardice. Not to give to charity is stingy, yet to hand out money to everyone who asks is profligate. Living among those who care about virtue, a child learns attentiveness to the quantities, modes and qualities of moral response that will enable her to locate the mean when it is her turn to decide. In this way, two of the three components that accompany Aristotle's understanding of a moral action – the action itself, and the appropriate feeling while doing it – are acquired through the influence of family and society, and the early acquisition of good habits.

The third component of a moral choice is the role of reason, and this requires the agent's self-conscious intent to be good. Good moral judgment requires a combination of education and directed experience. Herodotus' *History* illustrates that failure and success each have something to teach us as we build good moral judgment. Cadets I have worked with at the Air Force Academy frequently praise officers who let them fail, officers who can create controlled environments in which cadets could experience and come to understand their own mistakes. At St. John's College, faculty members teaching freshmen classes understand the importance of maintaining a silent, supervisory presence in the seminar while the students figure out for themselves how to work together. In Book One of Plato's *Republic*, Socrates' companions force the rebellious Thrasymachus to stay and learn from the experience of Socrates' cross-questioning.

Although good judgment is necessary if one is to exhibit the virtues of character, such judgment has to be distinguished from the behaviors that result from it: our actions and our emotions. Aristotle solves the problem of this distinction between thought, action, and behavior without resorting to Plato's rigid duality between body and mind. Good judgment is one of five types of thought-process that Aristotle names the virtues of thought. The extension of virtue to our mental processes is a lovely and unique feature of Aristotle's moral philosophy, and one that enables him to ensure that the would-be moral agent must expend considerable mental effort in the development of mature virtue.

Where does good judgment fit in among Aristotle's five virtues of thought? Of the five, three relate to science. The first of these, understanding (*nous* in Greek), relates to the unchanging first principles of any science that need to be mastered before one can proceed. For example, one must understand the law of inertia in order to proceed in the science of physics. The second, scientific knowledge (*episteme* in Greek), is just what it sounds like, and results from training in the tenets of a particular field. The third, wisdom (*sophia* in Greek), is a combination of understanding and scientific knowledge, and is the enactment of Aristotle's insistence that human beings by nature long to learn and understand. This longing goes beyond the satisfaction of finding that one's experiment yielded the results one wanted for some technological development, which was Bacon's limited notion of science. Human beings long to understand the nature of things. By separating wisdom from its two components, Aristotle acknowledges that one might have one without the other. While an individual might acquire an understanding of the principles of many fields of science in an undergraduate program, she might not proceed to scientific knowledge gained through advanced study. Similarly, a student might acquire the technical knowledge of how to solve calculus problems without ever learning the principles of the calculus. The fourth of Aristotle's virtues of thought, craft knowledge (*techne* in Greek), is entirely in the domain of experience. Vocational training is not theoretical. All principles and equations are learned in order to apply them in action.

Good judgment (*phronesis* in Greek) is the only one of the five
virtues of thought that combines theoretical learning with experience. Aristotle defines good judgment as "a state grasping the
truth, involving reason, concerned with action about things that are
good or bad for a human being" (NE 1140b5-6). Good judgment
is the thought-process that enables us to achieve the active virtues,
those Aristotle calls the virtues of character. Good judgment "is
about human concerns, about things open to deliberation" (NE
1141b10). In its theoretical component, it is concerned with human
values, our reasoned beliefs (1140b26-28) about society, politics,
and human conduct, conveyed not by a technical education, but
by the humanities. Because of its experiential component, good
judgment cannot simply be attained by study. Aristotle says, "it is
unclear what it requires," and as a result it is hard to find among the
young. "Whereas young people become accomplished in geometry
and mathematics, and wise within these limits," Aristotle observes,
"prudent young people do not seem to be found" (NE 1142a14-16).

All of this emphasis on human development results from Aristotle's conviction that human beings are teleological. Teleological
means "goal directed," and derives from the Greek word *telos*, which
means "end" or "goal." Everything we do deliberately, we do for
some goal. Getting up in the morning, eating breakfast, driving to
work, building a machine – such activities are undertaken because
they are means toward an end. Aristotle establishes this teleological aspect of human life as the basis for ethics in the opening line
of the *Nicomachean Ethics*: "Every craft and every line of inquiry,
and likewise every action and decision seems to seek some good"
(NE 1094a1). Our choices as to what goals we pursue are driven by

what we understand to be good. If we are mistaken about what is good, we will make poor choices. The study of ethics is necessary in order to reflect on the nature of what is good, and thereby help us choose our goals wisely so that they result in moral outcomes, and we can attain happiness through our thriving in our environments.

Furthermore, our teleological human existence is grounded in the type of biological organisms we are. Biological existence is also teleological. The acorn seeks to become an oak. The rose bush seeks to produce roses. Children's bodies have the goal of growing larger. This external process of biological growth is paralleled by an internal process of ethical growth. We learn good habits so we will not harm others, and instead come to interact successfully with them in families, communities, and states. As we grow, we optimally pay more and more attention to *why* these habits are important. Thus, we come to understand the principles behind good conduct, and ultimately are able to exhibit good character in its fullest sense, which for Aristotle is a necessary component of human thriving. This is the Aristotelian model of virtue. Good judgment is the mental virtue that extends to good decision-making, and is itself the goal of a long teleological process of biological and intellectual growth.

When we put Aristotle's definition of good judgment alongside his emphasis that the *orthos logos* cannot be prescriptive, moral judgment emerges looking more like an art than a science. While Plato insisted that good judgment was a purely rational matter, Aristotle's view has been the subject of much academic debate. The philosopher Martha Nussbaum argues that Aristotle's understanding of good judgment does not meet the criteria of science for several reasons, and furthermore, that nothing is to be gained by treating it as though it were. "Is practical reasoning scientific?" Nussbaum asks. "If it is not, as it is ordinarily practiced, can it be made to be? And would it be a good thing if it were?"[11] Nussbaum argues that the answer to all these questions is no. Aristotle does not present a single metric or quality according to which judgment can calculate the relative quantities present in the diverse options. Although Plato wished to place it within the domain of the universal, for Aristotle, judgment is only partially concerned with universals, and even there not universal knowledge, but universal belief. Finally, Aristotle rejects the Platonic notion that intellect alone can lead one to good choice. Our emotions are woven into our assessment of the relative goods from which we must choose, as are the appetites. Similarly, our previous actions play a role, setting up practical precedents and shaping our impressions of success and failure.

If good judgment is not wholly within the domain of reason, what is the value of education in developing the moral sense? By the terms of Aristotle's theory, moral education cannot be technical, for there are no universal rules for virtue, but only guiding principles. Moral education is the domain of the interpretive arts. The role of a liberal arts education is to instill an internal guide, developed by a dialogic interaction with a wide array of texts, in order to acquire the sense of context that will fulfill the requirements of *orthos logos*: to act in the right way, at the right time, in the right spirit, and with the right intent. While the *orthos logos* is a rational guide, its very formulation acknowledges that the irrational factors of chance and

---

11 Nussbaum, Martha. 2000. "The Discernment of Perception: An Aristotelian Conception of Private and Public Rationality." In *Aristotle's Ethics: Critical Essays*. Edited by Nancy Sherman. Lanham: Rowman and Littlefield Press, 145-182.

circumstance have a lot to do with whether an individual will locate the mean between the extremes and choose rightly.

Aristotle discusses the ongoing role of contingent external factors, which prevent virtue from being a completely reliable pathway to happiness. Fortune dispenses many external goods and ills, such as health or illness, wealth or poverty. Nonetheless, virtuous activity brings its own pleasure, which bad luck can diminish but not altogether take away. From observation, Aristotle concludes that morality cannot be a science, for knowledge of virtue is never valued as highly as virtue actively displayed in good conduct. As Aristotle says, "no [other] human achievement has the stability of activities in accord with virtue, since these seem to be more enduring even than our knowledge of the sciences" (NE 1100b12-15).

Aristotle offers a reminder that the love of the good is the most enduring human possession, with a longevity that outlasts scientific certainty, material success, and technological improvements to the material quality of life, those modern, humanitarian benefits for which we are indebted to the scientific revolution that Francis Bacon and René Descartes engineered. As we enjoy these benefits of quality of life in contemporary society, we must not forget to look back to the Greeks for a timeless and much-needed model of humanism that will help us make holistic decisions that honor all of the ways in which we are human.

Conclusion

It is appropriate to conclude a study of Greek humanism with Aristotle, who insists that humanity has to identify its highest goods and goals, not through the application of pure intellect to the problem, but in the midst of the messy real world. Aristotle views humans as being in constant interaction with the shifting variables of our natural, social, and political environment, and locates our decision-making processes and strategic thinking in the midst of this interaction. The Cartesian notion that we can attain an objective perspective from which to view and solve a strategic problem is often an illusion. It is in the quality of our interaction with our specific circumstances that the ethical caliber of our decisions emerge. Our age of unprecedented challenges needs more than ever a holistic model for strategic thinking that will build creative, flexible, and thoughtful agency oriented toward human thriving. Greek humanism offers us many valuable lessons as we aspire to such a model.

Leaders in our times need to have a wide range of tools to appreciate the choices available to them, and we have seen that Aristotle's *Nicomachean Ethics* is an excellent source for the skills of effective deliberation and decision-making. Aristotle appreciates that human reason operates in the midst of the fundamentally goal directed nature of human life. As we become attentive to the way we move around in our environments, pursuing goals that we decide on for various reasons, we begin to understand our orientation toward the complex and often overlapping interests of our appetites, our passions, and our reason. Ethics for Aristotle is the study of this fundamental feature of the human condition, in an effort to ascertain which of our goals are goods really worth having, and which merely seem to be good. This study does not happen in an isolated, hyper-rational environment, but in the midst of a full human life.

As we have seen, Aristotle resists the rationalism that characterized his teacher Plato's approach in favor of an approach that balances human reason, emotion, ambition, and love of virtue. Appropriate human response to human problems requires for Aristotle a consideration of rational and irrational factors alike. The essays here have shown that this spirit of Greek humanism remains profoundly relevant to our age, which takes to excess its faith in modern science to improve the human condition through technocratic means.

In separating scientific reason from its human context, Bacon and Descartes initiated the modern mindset that holds quantitative certainty as the highest goal of human knowledge. The technologies we have developed through modern science have liberated our physical bodies from the necessities of the real, natural world to an extraordinary extent. Yet they have done so by subordinating contemplation, which Aristotle considered the highest pursuit, to the necessity of making use of things. As we race to develop autonomous systems that will do our deciding for us, we overlook the ways in which the full array of human capacities is diminished in such a technocracy. While our technical capacities improve, the technocratic paradigm that develops them impoverishes our ability to embrace the full potential of our human existence. The Greek authors presented here show us how to recover an integrated view of the human being.

Aristotle's goal-directed foundation for ethical reflection grounds morality in our biological way of being in the world. As organisms, we experience a biological purposiveness as we go through the stages of life. Human reason for Aristotle is always situated in our particularly human way of being in the world, in which our development unfolds over time and space. Reflection on our biological situation offers a necessary antidote to the technological paradigms prevalent today that incline people to adopt a view of the human being that is divorced from its biological reality. Amidst this technocratic landscape, we need to pay particular attention to the quality of human judgment, which can be compromised and diminished as technologies emerge to make decisions for us. The Aristotelian teleological model can help us recognize the ways we allow the technocratic paradigm to dominate, and thus liberate human judgment to reflect strategically on what we are doing.

The Greek humanism I have laid forth here is not intended in an anti-technological spirit. Our dialogue about the human condition in our current technocracy should never be reduced to the binary choice between asserting a pro-technology or anti-technology stance. Technology brings enormous potential to human affairs. But with this potential comes an obligation to deliberate about what we most desire ethically, politically, militarily, socially, and individually. The Aristotelian model looks beyond merely tactical questions about how certain ends will be achieved, and reinforces the need for human judgment to do the work of engaging in deliberations about what ends are most desirable strategically for what they contribute to human flourishing. The strategists of tomorrow will need to factor into their deliberations an understanding of the full potential of human judgment. Aristotle codified his ethical model after Athenian society suffered a devastating defeat in a war that brought out human nature's worst tendencies toward violence and coercion. As our society faces complex threats to many aspects of human existence, we must reflect on the terms of our existence, and on the types of choices that will preserve the full array of human talent and potential.

The essays I have offered here show individuals whose diverse values and talents defined their active lives. These essays also illustrate an emerging awareness of what it means to be human. Homer's heroes struggled to find human meaning in a world they saw as largely fated. For the Homeric heroes, it is love of honor that drives them to the killing fields of war. These warriors show us the intensity of striving that characterizes human existence. Yet Homer also teaches us to notice the arena of human contest, the *agon*, the ground on which humans come together in order to compete and prove their merit. What in Homer manifests as a contest to the death on the battlefield becomes in later Greek literature a political arena in which humans can contest for honor, reputation, and prestige with non-fatal and hopefully productive consequences.

Herodotus shows us the process by which humanity emerged in the West from its sense of itself as fated. Herodotus' early characters are striving to liberate themselves from fate. Croesus attempted to take control of his destiny, but failed to exhibit the art of interpretation, and interpreted an ambiguous oracle through the lens of his own desire. His conqueror, Cyrus, was better equipped to navigate an ambiguous world, and understood that language has many levels of meaning. While Persian power was solidified under Cyrus, the Greeks were learning similar lessons about language and meaning. The Greeks, however, show how a love of freedom inspired experimentation with democratic governance, and a political model in which the most persuasive candidate would accede to political office. In such a democratic political contest, failure no longer needed to mean death. The Greek example suggests that failure may teach us far more valuable lessons than success ever could. In this context of the political arena, the individual learns to assess a situation holistically. Such an assessment requires more than a mere computation of data. It requires a synthesis of facts and impressions, an evaluation of our own and others' spiritedness, intentions, ambitions, and unstated desires. Cartesian data-sets cannot replace human judgement, poised as it is to evaluate rational and irrational factors holistically.

The Greeks illustrate a historical phenomenon that is true of the United States of America and many other nations as well, namely that it is through war that these people learned who they are. Until the Persian invasions, the Greeks did not share a sense of national identity. Only when they were tasked with working together for defense of all of Hellas, did the Greek-speaking peoples develop the sense that they owed allegiance to their homeland as a whole. Thucydides shows us how the Athenians learned in the Peloponnesian War the bitter truth of their own capacity for the imperialism and hubris that had doomed the Persian invasion half a century before. In the United States, the Revolutionary War honed our love of freedom and defined our distinct sovereignty, while the Civil War illustrated just how far people would go to protect the injustice of slavery.

After Athenian democracy devolved into political hubris and mob rule, Greek thinkers like Aristotle continued to work from the premise that human beings love the good, and can learn to make choices that are not just materially effective, but moral as well. Aristotle gives us a model for good judgement that occupies the center of moral choice. Such judgement proceeds from a rational framework of values, yet calibrates conduct according to each situation. Such a situational ethics can never be reduced to a single or simple rule. A human being cultivates this ethic through the course of a lifetime, hoping to learn from misjudgments and grow more adept at calibrating her conduct to meet what her circumstances demand. While our age may complicate this situational basis for ethical decision-making, this complexity makes the demand for such holistic judgment more imperative than ever.

Greek humanism also reminds us how deeply leadership and strategic thinking are rooted in language and reason, the Greek *logos*. The Greek heroes and politicians we have studied here remind us that we shape our social and political environments through our use of language. Language is a fundamental form of *techne*, a basic technology that frames our world. Without a love of virtue, language can easily become a tool of force. As Herodotus and Thucydides illustrate, persuasion as a mere political tool perpetrates profound injustice. Only with the checks and balances of our moral capacity to contemplate virtue and good character can persuasion become a tool for the good.

In this respect, Greek humanism offers many lessons we need to learn. Like the Greeks, intoxicated by their discovery of their own power, we too can become immersed in our technological prowess, and cannot always see for what they are its effects on our ways of being human. Just as the Athenians could not contain their own 'love of more,' we also can be seduced by passion and power, and surrender our own good judgment about far-reaching human ends. Our principles can be corroded, not only by the traditional pressures of external adversity, but by the often incremental and subtle ways that the technocratic paradigm narrows the range of human judgment. Aristotle reminds us that it is our responsibility to retain control of our cultural trajectory. In order to do this, we need to see the workings of own culture as something to be studied and understood. The study of the Greeks can help us locate our own culture, by showing us similarities and differences that we can only recognize by contrast.

These studies of Greek humanism show us how our thoughtful and creative Western forebears found their way to a remarkable model of effective strategy. This holistic way of approaching strategic thinking emphasizes language and reason utilized not in isolation from the physical factors of bodily life, but in embrace of the full diversity of these factors. Aristotelian morality does not pit itself against the appetites and passions, but urges that they be experienced in moderation. The Greek examples set out here are models for the importance of harnessing both the rational and irrational aspects of our nature, in order to direct them toward outcomes we can identify as desirable for their own sake, not as merely apparent goods, but as the proper ends for human endeavor. The world needs such thoughtful strategists more than ever, as our age faces unprecedented challenges, and stands in need of creative, flexible, strategic humanists.

Bibliography

Abrams, David. 1997. *The Spell of the Sensuous.* New York: Vintage Press.

Adkins, A. W. H. 1960. *Merit and Responsibility: A Study in Greek Values.* Oxford: Clarendon Press.

Anchor, Robert. 1967. *The Enlightenment Tradition.* Berkeley: University of California Press.

Anderson, Donald. 2008. "A Boatman's Story." In *When War Becomes Personal: Soldiers' Accounts From the Civil War to Iraq.* Iowa City: University of Iowa Press.

Aristotle. 1999. *Nicomachean Ethics.* Translated by Terence Irwin. Indianapolis: Hackett Publishing Company.

Bacon, Francis. 1999. "Preface," *The Great Instauration,* and *New Organon.* In *Selected Philosophical Works.* Edited by Rose-Mary Sargent. Indianapolis: Hackett Publishing Company.

Benardete, Seth. 2009. *Herodotean Inquiries.* South Bend: St. Augustine's Press.

Bethel, Scott, Prupas, Aaron, Ruby, Tomislav and Michael Smith. 2010. "Change Culture, Reverse Careerism." *Joint Forces Quarterly* 58, 3rd quarter 2010: 82-88.

Beyerchen, Alan. 1992. "Clausewitz, Nonlinearity and the Unpredictability of War." *International Security* 17.3: 59-90.

Bloom, Allan. 1968. *The Republic of Plato.* New York: Harper Collins.

Brookhiser, Richard. 1997. *Founding Father: Rediscovering George Washington.* New York: Free Press.

Choy, Yee Keong. 2018. "Cost-benefit Analysis, Values, Wellbeing and Ethics: An Indigenous Worldview Analysis." In *Ecological Economics* issue 145. Cambridge, MA: Elsevier Press.

Cialdini, Robert. 2009. *Influence: Science and Practice.* Boston: Allyn & Bacon.

Clancy, Tom. 1990. *The Hunt for Red October.* New York: Berkley Publishing Group.

Cloud, David and Greg Jaffe. 2010. *The Fourth Star: Four Generals and the Epic Struggle for the Future of the United States Army*. New York: Broadway Books.

Darley, J. M., and C. D. Batson. 1973. ""From Jerusalem to Jericho": A study of Situational and Dispositional Variables in Helping Behavior," *Journal of Personal and Social Psychology* 27: 100-108.

Descartes, René. 1985. *Discourse on the Method* and *Rules for the Direction of the Mind*. In *The Philosophical Writings of Descartes*. Translated by Cottingham, Stoothoff, and Murdoch. Cambridge: Cambridge University Press.

Dodds, E. R. 1951. *The Greeks and the Irrational*. Berkeley: University of California Press.

Eisenhower, Dwight. "Farewell Address." 17 January, 1961. https://www.ourdocuments.gov/doc.php?doc=90&page=transcript

George, Alexander and Richard Smoke. 1974. *Deterrence in American Foreign Policy*. New York: Columbia University Press.

Godwin, Doris Kearns. 2005. *Team of Rivals: The Political Genius of Abraham Lincoln*. New York: Simon & Schuster.

Gray, J. Glenn. 1998. *The Warriors, Reflections on Men in Battle*. Lincoln: Bison Books.

Hamilton, Alexander, Jay, John, and James Madison. 2001. *The Federalist*. Edited by George W. Carey and James McClellan. Carmel: Liberty Fund Books.

Hanson, Victor Davis. 1999. *The Soul of Battle*. New York: Simon & Schuster.

Hedges, Chris. 2014. *War is a Force that Gives Us Meaning*. New York: PublicAffairs.

Heidegger, Martin. 2019. *Being and Time*. Translated by John Macquarrie and Edward Robinson. New York: Harper & Row.

Hemingway, Ernest. 1925. "Soldier's Home." https://www.somanybooks.org/eng208/SoldiersHome.pdf

Herodotus. 1987. *The History*. Translated by David Grene. Chicago: University of Chicago Press.

Hill, Christopher. 2010. *Grand Strategies: Literature, Statecraft, and World Order*. New Haven: Yale University Press.

Hirst, Paul. 2015. *War and Power in the 21ˢᵗ Century*. Cambridge: Polity Press.

Homer. 1990. *The Iliad*, Translated by Robert Fagles. New York: Viking Penguin.

Hume, David. 1978. *A Treatise of Human Nature*. Edited by P. H. Nidditch. Oxford: Oxford University Press.

Huntington, Samuel. 2011. *The Clash of Civilizations*. New York: Simon & Schuster.

Ignatieff, Michael. 1998. *The Warrior's Honor: Ethnic War and the Modern Conscience*. New York: Holt Paperbacks.

Jervis, Robert, Lebow, Richard Ned, and Janice Gross Stein. 1989. *Psychology and Deterrence*. Baltimore: Johns Hopkins University Press.

Kagan, Donald. 1969. *The Outbreak of the Peloponnesian War*. Ithaca: Cornell University Press.

Kant, Immanuel. 2015. *Critique of Practical Reason*. Translated by Mary Gregor. Cambridge: Cambridge University Press.

—. 1993. *Grounding in the Metaphysics of Morals*. Translated by James Ellington. Indianapolis: Hackett Publishing Company.

—. 2017. *The Metaphysics of Morals*. Translated by Mary Gregor. Cambridge: Cambridge University Press.

Kaplan, Robert. 2007. "A Historian for Our Time." *The Atlantic*, Jan/Feb 2007. https://www.theatlantic.com/magazine/archive/2007/01/a-historian-for-our-time/305562/

—. 2002. *Warrior Politics: Why Leadership Demands a Pagan Ethos*. New York: Vintage Books.

Keats, John. 1817. "Letter to his brother." Web.

Keegan, John. 1976. *The Face of Battle*. London: Penguin Books.

Kerferd, G. B.. 1981. *The Sophistic Movement*. Cambridge: Cambridge University Press.

Kilcullen, David. 2010. *Counterinsurgency*. Oxford: Oxford University Press.

Kilcullen, David. 2006. "Twenty-Eight Articles," *Small Wars Journal*, summer 2006, article 13, (Build Trusted Networks). smallwarsjournal.com/documents/28 articles.pdf.

Kohllmann, Benjamin. 2012. "The Military Needs More Disruptive Thinkers." *Small Wars Journal*, 5 April 2012. Web.

Krüger, Gerhard. 2007. "The Origin of Philosophical Self-Consciousness." In *The New Yearbook for Phenomenology and Phenomenological Philosophy* Volume 7: 200-259.

Lebow, Richard Ned. 2007. "Thucydides and Deterrence." *Security Studies* 16:2: 163-188.

Lefkowitz, Mary. 2003. *Greek Gods, Human Lives: What We can Learn from Myths.* New Haven: Yale University Press.

Liddell, Henry George and Robert Scott. 2019. *Greek-English Lexicon.* Oxford: Clarendon Press.

McDowell, John. 1979. "Virtue and Reason." In *Aristotle's Ethics: Critical Essays.* Edited by Nancy Sherman. Lanham: Rowman and Littlefield Press, 121-144.

McMasters, H. R.. 1997. *Dereliction of Duty.* New York: HarperCollins.

McPherson, James. 1997. *For Cause and Comrades: Why Men Fought in the Civil War.* Oxford: Oxford University Press.

—. 2008. *Tried by War: Abraham Lincoln as Commander in Chief.* London: Penguin Books.

Momigliano, A. D.. 1966. "Some Observations on Causes of War in Ancient Historiography." In *Studies in Historiography.* London: University of London Press.

Montaigne, Michel. 1958. *The Complete Essays of Montaigne.* Translated by Donald M. Frame. Stanford: Stanford University Press.

Morrison, James. 2006. *Reading Thucydides.* Columbus: The Ohio State University Press.

Nagel, Thomas. 1987. "War and Massacre." In *Moral Philosophy: Selected Reading.* Edited by George Shor. San Diego: Harcourt Brace Jovanovich.

Nagy, Gregory. 1979. *The Best of the Achaeans.* Baltimore: The Johns Hopkins University Press.

Niebuhr, Reinhold. 2008. *The Irony of American History.* Chicago: University of Chicago Press.

Nussbaum, Martha. 2000. "The Discernment of Perception: An Aristotelian Conception of Private and Public Rationality." In *Aristotle's Ethics: Critical Essays.* Edited by Nancy Sherman. Lanham: Rowman and Littlefield Press, 145-182.

Ong, Walter J. 1988. *Orality and Literacy: The Technologizing of the Word*. London: Methuen Books.

Orwin, Clifford. 1994. *The Humanity of Thucydides*. Princeton: Princeton University Press.

Paul, T. V., Morgan, Patrick and James Wirtz, editors. *Complex Deterrence: Strategy in the Global Age*. Chicago: University of Chicago Press.

Payne, Keith. 2001. *The Fallacies of Cold War Deterrence and a New Direction*. Lexington: University Press of Kentucky.

Plato. 1961. *Symposium*. In *The Collected Dialogues of Plato*. Edited by Edith Hamilton and Huntington Cairns. Princeton: Princeton University Press.

Plutarch, 2001. "Life of Alexander," in *Plutarch's Lives Volume II*. Translated by John Dryden. New York: Modern Library.

—. 1965. *Moralia, Volume XI: On the Malice of Herodotus. Causes of Natural Phenomena*. Translated by Lionel Pearson and F. H. Sandbach. Cambridge, MA: Harvard University Press.

Reiman, Saara. 2009. "Is Space an Environment?" In *Space Policy* issue 25. Cambridge, MA: Elsevier Press.

Ricks, Thomas. 2006. *Fiasco: The American Military Adventure in Iraq*. London: Penguin Press.

Rousseau, Jean-Jacques. 1966. "Essay on the Origin of Languages." in *On the Origin of Language*. Translated by John Moran and Alexander Gode. Chicago: University of Chicago Press.

Ryle, Gilbert. 2000. *The Concept of Mind*. Chicago: University of Chicago Press.

Said, Edward. 1981. *Covering Islam: How the Media and the Experts Determine How We See the Rest of the World*. New York: Pantheon Books.

Shay, Jonathan. 1994. *Achilles in Vietnam: Combat Trauma and the Undoing of Character*. New York: Scribner Books.

—. 1991. "Learning about Combat Stress from Homer's *Iliad*," *Journal of Traumatic Stress*, 4.4, 561-579.

Sherman, Nancy. 1989. *The Fabric of Character: Aristotle's Theory of Virtue*. Oxford: Clarendon Press.

—. 2010. *The Untold War: Inside the Hearts, Minds, and Souls of our Soldiers*. New York: W. W. Norton & Company.

Sherman, William. 2013. *Memoirs of General W. T. Sherman*. CreateSpace Independent Publishing Platform.

Simpson, Peter and Robert French. 2006. "Negative Capability and the Capacity to Think in the Present Moment: Some Implications for Leadership Practice." *Leadership* 2.2: 245-55.

Sophocles. 2013. *Antigone*. In *Antigone, Oedipus the King, Oedipus at Colonus*. Edited by David Grene and Richmond Lattimore. Translated by Elizabeth Wyckoff. Chicago: University of Chicago Press.

Ste. Croix, G. E. M. 1972. *The Origins of the Peloponnesian War*. Ithaca: Cornell University Press.

Stein, Janice. 2009. "Rational Deterrence against "Irrational" Adversaries." In *Complex Deterrence: Strategy in the Global Age*. Edited by T. V. Paul, Patrick Morgan, and James Wirtz. Chicago: University of Chicago Press.

Strassler, Robert. 2009. *The Landmark Herodotus*. New York: Anchor Books.

—. 1998. *The Landmark Thucydides: A Comprehensive Guide to the Peloponnesian War*. New York: Free Press.

Thucydides. 1998. *The Peloponnesian War*. Translated by Steven Lattimore. Indianapolis: Hackett Press.

Turner, Brian. 2005. "The Hurt Locker." https://www.poetryfoundation. org/poems/54141/the-hurt-locker

Valery, Paul. 1978. "Une vue de Descartes," *Variete V*. Paris: Site Gallimard.

von Clausewitz, Carl. 1991. *On War*. Translated by J. J. Graham. Web.

Volk, Katherina. 2002. "Kleos Aphthitos Revisited." *Classical Philology* 97.1: 61-68.

Voltaire. 1961. *Philosophical Letters*, Translated by Ernest Delworth. Indianapolis: Bobbs-Merrill Company.

Walzer, Michael. 1977. *Just and Unjust Wars*, 4th edition. New York: Basic Books.

Weil, Simone. 1965. "The Iliad, or the Poem of Force." *Chicago Review* 18.2: 5-30.

Zagorin, Peter. 2005. *Thucydides: An Introduction for the Common Reader*. Princeton: Princeton University Press.

Index